ATHLETE IS AGENDER

ATHLETE IS AGENDER

TRUE STORIES OF LGBTQ+ PEOPLE IN SPORTS

EDITED BY

KATHERINE LOCKE
AND **NICOLE MELLEBY**

ART BY **JESS VOSSETEIG**

Christy Ottaviano Books

LITTLE, BROWN AND COMPANY
New York   Boston

ABOUT THIS BOOK

The illustrations for this book were done digitally. This book was edited by Jessica Anderson and designed by Jenny Kimura and Carla Weise. The production was supervised by Jonathan Lopes, and the production editor was Marisa Finkelstein. The text was set in Sabon LT Std, and the display type is KG Inimitable Original Regular.

Christy Ottaviano Books
Hachette Book Group
1290 Avenue of the Americas, New York, NY 10104
Visit us at LBYR.com

First Edition: May 2025

Christy Ottaviano Books is an imprint of Little, Brown and Company. The Christy Ottaviano Books name and logo are registered trademarks of Hachette Book Group, Inc.

The publisher is not responsible for websites (or their content) that are not owned by the publisher.

Little, Brown and Company books may be purchased in bulk for business, educational, or promotional use. For information, please contact your local bookseller or the Hachette Book Group Special Markets Department at special.markets@hbgusa.com.

Library of Congress Cataloging-in-Publication Data
Names: Locke, Katherine, editor. | Melleby, Nicole, editor. | Vosseteig, Jess, illustrator.
Title: Athlete is agender : true stories of LGBTQ+ people in sports / edited by Katherine Locke, Nicole Melleby ; art by Jess Vosseteig.
Other titles: True stories of LGBTQ+ people in sports
Description: First edition. | New York : Little, Brown and Company, 2025. | Includes bibliographical references. | Audience: Ages 9–14 | Summary: "A groundbreaking nonfiction collection of well-known LGBTQ professional athletes and queer authors telling stories about the feeling of belonging that comes with finding a sport that's yours, all dynamically packaged with photographs and full-color interior illustrations." —Provided by publisher
Identifiers: LCCN 2024042657 | ISBN 9780316572002 (hardcover) | ISBN 9780316572019 (ebook)
Subjects: LCSH: Gay athletes—Juvenile literature. | Transgender athletes—Juvenile literature.
Classification: LCC GV708.8 .A845 2024 | DDC 796.092/66—dc23/eng/20241017
LC record available at https://lccn.loc.gov/2024042657

ISBNs: 978-0-316-57200-2 (paper over board), 978-0-316-57201-9 (ebook)

PRINTED IN DONGGUAN, CHINA

APS

10 9 8 7 6 5 4 3 2 1

For all the queer and trans athletes
who have made their sport their home,
we're cheering for you.
—KL & NM

CONTENTS

INTRODUCTION

Sports have always given us what we needed, exactly when we needed it—whether we were aware at the time or not.

For Nicole, it turns out the sports she played when she was younger were full of queer kids who had somehow come together as a team without knowing what they might have in common. Something about those team sports—basketball, softball, field hockey—offered its own comfort of found family. And for Katherine, it's clear—in retrospect—why they gravitated to equestrian sports, the only Olympic events where all genders compete equally against one another.

It's no surprise that queer kids find safety in sports, and not just in team sports. Swimming, sailing, cycling, martial arts, and a wealth of other activities often help queer kids feel free and safe enough to release physical energy, frustration, and ever-growing confusion, in a forum where it's not only cathartic but encouraged.

According to a survey conducted by The Trevor Project, although nearly one in three lesbian, gay, bisexual, transgender, and queer or questioning (LGBTQ+) young people reported participating in sports, a number of LGBTQ+ youth said they chose not to because of discrimination or fear. For queer kids, belonging to a sport can feel like home, but it's still something we're constantly fighting for. More and more, transgender athletes are being banned and scrutinized, toxic masculinity in male sports makes it difficult for queer boys and men to feel safe enough to come out, and sports tend to be separated into male or female, making it hard for non-binary athletes to find their place. Sometimes queer kids who belong to one sport find themselves abandoning it for another because of these restrictive gender norms and rules.

There's something inherently powerful about under-mining stereotypes. About celebrating queer kids as strong, athletic champions on the field, in the rink, or in the pool. There's something uniquely special about witnessing a player use they/them pronouns on an Olympic field, or watching two married teammates win a WNBA championship, or watching a soccer player open up, despite the toxic culture of his sport, to say, "I'm gay."

We are everywhere, we deserve to be everywhere, and we can excel everywhere.

Each contributor in *Athlete Is Agender* understands this deeply. They've all found a safe home in their sport, and sometimes that means they've had to fight for their place in it. While these contributors are out and proud members of the LGBTQ+ community, being a queer athlete in no way means you need to feel pressure to be out, or to be a public figure or role model. Knowing that it brings you joy to put on a base-ball mitt, or to tie up your running shoes for a race, or to sit on the bench and cheer for your teammates, or to climb on that horse…those are the things that matter. You matter.

Athlete is agender. Athlete can mean *anyone*.

The athletes in these pages span all types of sports. In creating this book, we did our best to feature as many different identities and sports as possible, including football, basketball, baseball, dog sledding, equestrian sports, sailing, water aerobics, archery, tennis, figure skating, and swimming. Some sports are missing—not because they don't have queer representation but because all books are finite. It's important to remember that every sport has featured queer players since its invention, and queer people can participate in any sport. Sports are for everybody and every body.

Whoever you are or might be, on the field and in your heart, we're proud of you. Let's get out there and do our best, team.

—Katherine Locke and Nicole Melleby

A NOTE ON PRONOUNS

PRONOUN (NOUN)

1. any of a small set of words (such as *I, she, he, you, it, we, or they*) in a language that are used as substitutes for nouns or noun phrases and whose referents are named or understood in the context

2. the third-person personal pronouns (such as *he/him, she/her,* and *they/them*) that a person goes by

—*Merriam-Webster.com Dictionary*

WHY ARE PRONOUNS IMPORTANT?

After doing a large study, researchers at the University of Texas found that when transgender youths are allowed to use their chosen names in places such as at work, school, and home, their risk of depression and suicide drops.

This means that it is essential to learn and respect the pronouns of your fellow teammates and peers. You can't know a person's pronouns just by looking at them, and you don't want to single anyone out by only asking for their pronouns, either. The best course of action is to always be mindful and ask everyone what their pronouns are. That way, you set up a safe space right from the start, letting your team and opposing athletes know that you support them for who they are.

Keep in mind that sometimes you or someone else might not be comfortable sharing their pronouns, and that's okay, too! You can always refer to that person by their name.

WHAT IS MISGENDERING?

When someone is misgendered, that means that they are referred to as a gender that they don't identify with. This could be done by using the wrong pronouns; addressing a group of people by saying, "Hey, guys!" or "Hey, ladies!"; or by making assumptions about someone's gender because of the way they look or act.

Try to use gender-neutral phrases when talking to your teammates, such as:

"Hey, batter, batter!"

"Nice shot, Number 22!"

"You've got this, team!"

If you unintentionally misgender someone, know that mistakes sometimes happen. The respectful thing to do is apologize, correct yourself, and learn.

And if you hear someone intentionally misgendering a teammate or peer, speak up! Being a good ally is important.

Want to know more about how to be a good teammate and ally? Turn to page 193 for some ideas.

MOST COMMONLY USED PRONOUNS:

He/him	Xe/xir
She/her	All pronouns
They/them	No pronouns (use their name)
E/em	

This is not a complete list. Even if you've never heard of someone's pronouns before, it is still important to learn them, respect them, and use them.

Not sure about your own pronouns? You're not alone, and you're allowed to try one out and change your mind. You don't always need to know immediately which fits best for you, or you may decide to use more than one set of pronouns.

Remember: There's no right or wrong when it comes to navigating your identity.

★ ★ ★ ★ ★

WHAT IS TITLE IX? AND WHY DOES IT MATTER?

"No person in the United States shall, on the basis of sex, be excluded from participation in, be denied the benefits of, or be subjected to discrimination under any education program or activity receiving federal financial assistance."

—TITLE IX

THE HISTORY

Title IX is a civil rights law passed in 1972 with the aim of making sure girls received the same opportunities as boys in schools. Before Title IX, a female student like Bernice Sandler wasn't allowed to be a crossing guard or even run the slide projector at school. She also didn't have access to athletics in school. While boys had plenty of sports teams to choose from, girls were excluded from those teams, and they didn't have their own girls' teams to join, either.

As a young girl, Bernice didn't think she could do anything to change the status quo. But when she was denied a public-university teaching job as an adult on the basis of gender, she decided it was time to fight back.

Bernice started by researching strategies used by other civil rights activists. She came across an executive order written by President Lyndon B. Johnson in 1965, which stated that federally assisted employers could not discriminate based on race, color, religion, and national origin. In 1967, President Johnson added to the law: Employers could not discriminate against a person's gender, either.

Building off this executive order as well as the Civil Rights Act of 1964, Bernice worked with the Women's Equity Action League from 1969 to 1971 to file gender discrimination charges against 250 schools. In 1970, she filed a lawsuit against all universities in the United States.

Even though Bernice's lawsuits primarily targeted colleges and universities, the resulting Title IX legislation now also applies to elementary, middle, and high schools. From 1972 onward, girls were no longer forced to take classes like cooking, sewing, or typing, and could also learn to repair cars and build things in shop class. Any educational and recreational opportunities offered to boys were now offered to girls, too.

While the law wasn't written specifically with sports in mind, it's had a huge impact on athletics.

Before Title IX, only one in twenty-seven girls played sports. Today, that ratio is two in five.

But what exactly does Title IX *do*—and how does it benefit everyone?

FIVE THINGS TITLE IX DOES

1. Gives students of any gender equal access to all available school programs, including classes, extracurriculars, and sports. This does not just protect cisgender girls—it prohibits discrimination based on any gender identity and sexual orientation.

2. Requires schools to appoint a Title IX coordinator. This person (or group of people) is responsible for making sure the school always remains in compliance with the law.

3. Requires schools to create a policy stating that it does not discriminate on the basis of sex or gender in its educational programs and activities. This must be publicly published and widely available. Most schools include it in their student handbooks.

4. Requires schools to recognize and investigate all complaints of sexual or gender-based harassment or violence.

5. Requires schools to create a policy for students to file complaints of sex or gender discrimination. The policy must include procedures for addressing and resolving the complaints, and to ensure the students filing these complaints are not retaliated against in any way.

WHAT ABOUT TRANSGENDER ATHLETES?
DOES TITLE IX PROTECT THEM, TOO?

The U.S. Department of Education has told schools that Title IX protects students from discrimination based on gender identity.

In 2021, US Secretary of Education Miguel Cardona said, "The Supreme Court has upheld the right for LGBTQ+ people to live and work without fear of harassment, exclusion, and discrimination—and our LGBTQ+ students have the same rights and deserve the same protections. I'm proud to have directed the Office for Civil Rights to enforce Title IX to protect all students from all forms of sex discrimination."

TO FIND OUT MORE ABOUT TITLE IX,
VISIT THESE WEBSITES

United States Department of Justice—justice.gov

National Sexual Violence Resource Center—nsvrc.org

U.S. Department of Education—ed.gov

Don't forget to ask a teacher or administrator about the Title IX policy for your own school!

SPORTS AS CONFRONTATION AND CELEBRATION

BY MARIEKE NIJKAMP

WHAT IT FEELS LIKE TO BE EXCLUDED

It's a sunny summer afternoon in the mid-1990s. One of those days where the sky is vibrantly blue, the air feels hot and sticky, and no one cares, because you're ten or eleven and all that matters is the field around you, the rusty goal, and the soccer ball you're kicking around. The ball is halfway through falling apart, the stitches of the leather panels worn and fraying, but it's good for a few more games. The field is a patch of grass in the middle of a neighborhood where all the houses are small and worn, too, and everyone knows one another.

You don't remember whose ball it is or who started the game. It probably didn't even start as a game, just a handful of kids kicking at the goal. Then others joined in. Someone formed teams. Someone brought ice pops.

Marieke Nijkamp

"When I was growing up, summers were for soccer and swimming and trying out every ball game we could find." —Marieke Nijkamp

The boys and girls around you are calling out and laughing, and right here, right now, this is the most important game in the world. At least for a little while.

Until the sun burns even hotter, the ice pops are a distant memory, and the boys take off their shirts. It's normal for them. They're used to it, to the freedom of having the sun burn down on their backs and shoulders, while the grass tickles their feet.

And you don't think about it. You don't think about the fact that you're not a boy like them. You don't feel like you're a girl, either. You just want to play the game. (It will be *years* until you come across the word *nonbinary* and realize that's it. That is who you are. That is the word that fits you.) You don't think about the fact that you're eleven and your body is on the cusp of changing. You do the same as the boys. You take off your shirt.

And from one moment to the next, what was carefree isn't carefree anymore, but weighed down by stares and whispers and scorn. You don't understand what's wrong, and it will be a while before you do, because it doesn't *feel* wrong to play like the others. To play like yourself.

But right then and there, it only matters what other people think. Different. Uncomfortable. *Weird*. In this moment, the game doesn't belong to you anymore. Or perhaps it would be more accurate to say: You do not belong to it.

Sports and I, we've always had a complicated relationship. It's not just a question of gender, it's a question of (dis)ability, too. I've fallen in love with so many sports, both as a spectator and as an athlete. I've also had to let go of quite a few. So let me tell you about archery.

I don't quite remember how old I was when I tried archery for the first time, but it must have been around fourteen. I'd already tried other sports. Fencing, for a few weeks. Handball, for a few years, and always as goalkeeper. Soccer, again, but only at school. Rowing, for a hot minute, but it requires being comfortable in open water, and despite growing up in a country that mostly lies below sea level, I've never been a strong swimmer.

Trying on a new sport always meant trying to find a new balance with my body, with joints that refused to do as they were told, with chronic fatigue and pain, with limits. And while I was—and am—competitive, playing sports was never my whole life, just a part of it. Even if it was (and is) a pretty big part. Then came archery.

From the very first moment I held a bow, it felt like an extension of my arm. It felt like something I knew how to do and something I *should* do. I loved it. According to one of my first coaches, I was a natural talent. He saw me going to national and international competitions. Obviously, I loved that idea.

But I never got that far. Instead, I ended up with a double elbow injury. On both the inside of my elbow *and* the outside, the points where the tendon connects the muscle to the bone were injured, limiting my ability to use my hand and arm. Even after treatment and physical therapy, my right elbow remained a weak spot. I tried archery again after recovering, but the strain of drawing was too much. From that point on, I never got beyond recreational shooting. And, of course, the occasional ren fair.

It only occurred to me later that if I had been able to pursue competitive archery in some form, it would have meant competing in gendered categories. The 2020 Summer Olympics were the first with a mixed archery team, but

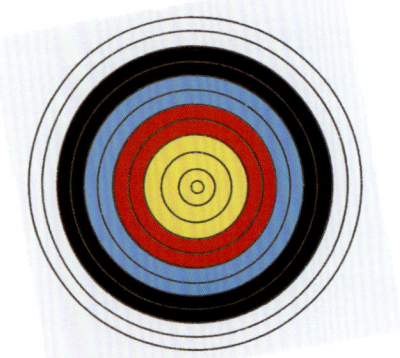

every official tournament is divided into women's archery and men's archery.

———

Pursuing this sport would have meant confining myself to a category I did not belong to, just to be able to fit in. In a strange and uncomfortable way, I felt lucky that I never had to make that choice. And I felt bad that I felt lucky.

———

When I finally came across the word *nonbinary*, it unlocked a part of me that I'd always known but never had language for. It fit me like a well-worn pair of boots, and I never wanted to take it off. Being nonbinary makes me feel more comfortably me. It makes me stand a little bit taller.

The idea that I would have had to set part of myself aside if I'd ever had the opportunity to compete in any of the sports I fell in love with still leaves me feeling sad and more than a little dysphoric. It's a cruel choice no one should ever have to make.

I am nonbinary. I love sports, with a passion. Both of those things should be cause for celebration, not confrontation.

And still, the confrontation is there. As a nonbinary person. As a queer person who—far too often—hears sports fans use *gay* as a slur. I see sports draw boundaries and lines in the sand. This is who does and doesn't belong. This is ours, not yours.

For most of the sports I love, the international organizations in charge have worked hard to create rules to exclude transgender and nonbinary athletes. I always wonder if they realize what it tells us. That the sport doesn't belong to us, or we to it.

I'd wish they'd write rules to include athletes, instead. Because they *can*. It's no easier to change the rules and regulations to *exclude* people than it is to change those same rules and regulations to *include* them. If we're all so afraid that something is unfair, we should work to make it fairer for all. Exclusion is never the only option; it's always a conscious choice. And we deserve better. We deserve more.

Because we belong here, too.

WHAT IT FEELS LIKE TO BELONG

It's a warm summer evening in the early 2020s. One of those evenings when the heat of the day is making way for the cooler colors of night, and everyone around you is singing to keep this moment going. To keep this soccer game going. You're all singing despite the fact that your team is losing.

Because sometimes, in true Olympic spirit, what matters most *isn't* winning—it's being present. Together. As supporters of a team that you've seen through ups and downs. And tonight your team is losing, but it doesn't matter because everyone on the pitch is giving their all and everyone around you is responding in kind.

So you sing and chant until your throat is sore. You look around and you feel the energy roll off the stands. And for a moment the outside world, crumbling and angry and hurt, feels distant. Your pain and limits don't matter. This is joy. Pure joy. As you carve out a little bit of space and celebrate everything that led you here.

Where you belong.

Sports have always been a part of me. Some of my earliest memories are sports related. I remember being tiny and staying at my grandparents' while my grandfather watched the Tour de France. Hours upon hours of men on bikes struggling up mountains and hurling themselves off again, mixed with endless helicopter views of the French landscape. I didn't have a clue back then that cycling was a team sport. Or that there was any sort of strategy to what those riders were doing. But

I was fascinated by it. To this day, there's still a small part of me that associates every Tour de France with that old, staticky television set, the smell of heavy wooden furniture and leather upholstery, and the scratchy pale couch where I used to sit and watch with my grandfather.

I remember iconic tennis matches on other couches. Long weekends watching speed skating. People huddled together to watch Olympic events at school, at college, later at work, even in public. Those moments when time stands still because everyone, everywhere, is watching the exact same thing.

I remember falling in love with soccer. First, because it's almost impossible to avoid in this soccer-obsessed country, where far too many people dress up in the most absurd, wonderful, ridiculous orange outfits during World Cups and European Championships. (Yes, me too. Begrudgingly.) Then, because I began to understand the game itself. The team spirit, the *stories*. The way soccer isn't just a sport, but a community. My club.

I wondered if I belonged at the stadium, because everyone who's ever been around European soccer supporters knows that they can be a rough crowd, and I'm a queer, blue-haired geek. But one day, I lucked into two tickets, and it felt like homecoming. I distinctly remember being so high up in the stadium, just about the farthest anyone could be from the pitch, when the people around me started to sing.

Now, I wish I could tell you that it was never rough and always welcoming. It wasn't and isn't. But I'd like to think, one day, it could be.

Maybe I'm naive. I've gotten into arguments with racists. I've called people out for using homophobic slurs. I've seen violence in the stands, and I've had to learn how to avoid it. But I've also seen people change their ways when challenged. I've seen people reconsider what they're saying and doing, even how they're thinking about others.

Over many years of being a soccer fan, I've always been surrounded by that same rough crowd. But I've managed to strike up conversations even with supporters from the opposing teams. We may not agree on club colors, but we speak the same common sports language. And through that shared language, we can learn to understand and respect one another.

I believe change is possible because I've seen it. And for all that sports are inherently about us versus them, this one always, *always*, simply starts with *us*.

Sports, to me as a storyteller, are about stories. A lost but celebrated match. A tennis player coming into a tournament on a wild card and taking home the trophy. A cyclist crashing off his bike and running up a mountain instead. A track athlete falling down, getting back up, and *winning*. A speed skater missing a lane change. A shared gold medal.

But above all, it's about community. The bonds that form when you fall in love with a game. The common language. The way you celebrate together when you win and mourn together when you lose. The texts my neighbor and I exchange after every game to make sure the other got home safe. The hours of conversations with friends as we watch sports together, even on different sides of the country or different sides of the world. Joy, passion, excitement.

At its best, sports bring people together, no exceptions. No exclusions.

Every sports fan I know doesn't just celebrate wins, but courage, too. And I remember all the moments of courage that made sports feel more welcoming and inclusive to me.

Queer athletes, like South African soccer player Phuti Lekoloane, coming out and paving the way, and reminding the rest of the world that we're here already—and we've always been.

Trans and nonbinary athletes, like Australian wheelchair racer Robyn Lambird, showing up and following their passions, despite the pushback, because sports belong to us, we belong to them, and we're not going anywhere.

Disabled athletes, like Dutch tennis player Esther Vergeer, showing all the ways in which sports can be expansive, inclusive, and here for every single one of us.

This is courage. These are the stories, the memories, the community. This is what we celebrate.

And one day, we will win.

FINDING MYSELF ON THE ICE

BY A. J. SASS

When I was a kid, my family moved from Omaha, Nebraska, to Rochester, Minnesota, and I was not thrilled about it.

One weekend, I was holed up in my new room reading when my mom knocked on my door.

"Hi, sweetie."

I could hear the smile in her voice, although I didn't look up. I still hadn't forgiven my parents for uprooting my entire life.

Ignoring my stony silence, Mom kept talking. "I thought it'd be nice for us to get out of the house and spend some time together as a family today."

This did *not* sound nice to me. But Mom was holding a set of tickets for a local ice-skating show.

I liked skating. Mom and I watched it on TV every chance we got, and my family had attended Ice Capades shows back in Omaha. I didn't say anything as I set down my book, but secretly I was excited.

Even still, I pretended to be grumpy on the drive to the local recreation center and stayed quiet as Mom and Dad bought pop, M&M's, and Twizzlers. I slouched once we found seats high up in the stands. At this point I still was trying hard not to seem excited.

But as soon as the spotlights blinked on and skaters streamed out in their glittery costumes, I sat up. I couldn't help bouncing my legs in time to the songs and clapping at the end of each number. Spellbound.

The show's theme was "United Skates." There was a group number performed to "Georgia on My Mind," a precision team skating to Kentucky bluegrass music, and a "Born in the U.S.A." solo number, among many others.

My favorite was the "New York, New York" number performed by a national-level competitor. She launched herself into jumps without any hesitation and spun so fast she became a blur under the spotlights. But it was her costume I loved most of all. While the other girls performed in sparkly dresses, this skater wore silver pants and a form-fitting black vest. I had *never* seen a girl skater in leggings or pants before. That afternoon, I imagined myself in her place, flying across the ice with an audience clapping for me, wearing that same costume.

As the show came to an end and spectators headed toward the exit, I turned to my parents.

"I want to learn to skate," I told them, "so I can be in this show next year."

Mom's lips twitched up at the corners, forming a smile. "I think we can make that happen."

Finally, I had something to be excited about in Rochester.

Skating quickly became a major part of my life. In many ways, it was also my refuge. As an autistic kid who struggled with making friends, I saw skating as something I could look forward to in the evenings after school. I progressed from one class per week to two, then three. I wasn't the fastest learner, but I loved getting to practice new skills until I mastered them.

It was also inspiring to watch the high-level skaters in the free-style session right before my class. At the time I began skating, Rochester was home to multiple national- and international-level competitors. I was especially starstruck by Olympian and Polish national champion Grzegorz Filipowksi, who lived on our street. I aspired to fly across the ice with the same speed as him, to launch into jumps with the same spring and agility.

While the girls in my skate school admired Nancy Kerrigan and Michelle Kwan, I wanted to skate just like Grzegorz Filipowksi.

One afternoon, I arrived at the rink to a group of skaters crowding around a display that held trophies, medals, and other awards earned by members of our club. But the kids weren't studying the display. They were focused on the wall next to it.

I came to a stop at the back of the crowd, next to a girl in my skating class. Even on my tiptoes, I still wasn't tall enough to see what everyone else did.

"They just posted the ice show cast list," she told me. "We get to see what music we'll be skating to!"

The crowd finally parted enough for us to weave our way to the front. I scanned the list, reading carefully until I saw Skate School Level 2: "9 to 5" by Dolly Parton.

My hands tingled with excitement. I could already imagine myself in a business suit, like what my dad wore to work. My thoughts took off from there. Maybe it'd be just like the costume that the "New York, New York" soloist had worn, except with black pants instead of silver. Maybe we'd get to wear ties lined with sparkling crystals. I smiled.

Beside me, my classmate squealed. "Look! There's our costume—isn't it cute?"

My gaze shifted to a big poster board displaying glossy dance catalog cutouts. But then I saw the costume she was pointing at: a yellow dress with '80s-style shoulder pads. The dress was lined with black sequins, the skirt shorter in the front and longer in the back. There was even a matching lacy hat pinned to one side of the model's head.

My smile dimmed.

A.J. Sass in costume for a Dolly Parton-themed ice show, 1993.

Before I could say anything, our skate school instructor called us to start class.

It was a relief to focus on something else. Because that bright, frilly dress wasn't even close to the costume I'd dreamed of performing in.

As I got older and continued to advance as a skater, I ran up against this tension again and again. No matter what I tried, I didn't quite fit in. While the girls in my skate school adored all our costumes, I felt an odd prickle of discomfort that I tried to ignore but couldn't quite shake. I also felt like someone else—not fully myself—whenever I wore makeup for shows and competitions.

It wasn't that I hated wearing costumes or makeup. Not exactly. My discomfort came from what people assumed about me when I dressed a certain way. Makeup, long hair, and skirts all automatically made people think *girl*. Even the color of my skates told people how to interpret my gender before I could tell them myself. Black skate boots were for boys, while white boots were for girls.

Despite feeling like I was playing a part meant for someone else, I loved skating. With my family's frequent relocations, it was one of the few consistencies in my life. We moved again after I started middle school, this time from Minnesota to Georgia, and skating was there, too. It welcomed me when I moved back to Minnesota at the beginning of high school. The sport became a lifeline as I struggled with anxiety after I skipped a grade and began attending college at fifteen.

Figure skating has come a long way since I was a kid, back when some rinks required skating dresses for girls during practices and competitions. The rules have since changed. Now all skaters can compete in leggings or bodysuits. In ice dance, the steps skaters can choose to perform for pattern dances have recently been renamed from "ladies" or "men" steps to "follow" or "lead" steps, allowing skaters more freedom, regardless of their gender.

I was still actively competing as an adult when I moved to California for graduate school. Once I settled into a new job and life in San Francisco, I started meeting other queer people for the first time and participating in support groups for folks who didn't feel like the sex they'd been assigned at birth aligned with their gender. Over several years, I took steps to become a more authentic version of myself: I cut my hair short, began to medically transition under the care of knowledgeable doctors, and updated my name and pronouns.

I was only skating occasionally by this point, without a coach. Coming out to friends and family and transitioning at work took up a lot of my mental energy. But once I'd gotten through the harder parts of my transition, I gravitated back toward the sport I loved. I found a supportive coach and began training more regularly again. I even passed my Senior Free Skate test (now called Gold Singles) and began dabbling in ice dance.

> **Returning to the rink also made me realize that while being seen as a man felt better than being seen as a woman, I still felt some discomfort related to my gender. And this confused me a lot: I'd already transitioned, and I did feel better, so now what?**

One day, a coach contacted me out of the blue to ask if I'd like to join her synchronized-skating team.

"I'm not sure," I initially responded.

Synchronized skating is a discipline where skaters perform a program by making formations as a group, as well as doing intersections and pairs moves. It is also coed, meaning both men and women can compete on the same team together. I'd been on a team as a teenager, but it was composed entirely of girls, and I'd run into the same discomfort with dresses and makeup that I had felt elsewhere in the sport.

"At least come try out next week and see what you think," the coach said before texting me a flyer.

A few days passed before I got around to looking at it. Eventually, I read the details.

One line immediately caught my eye:

ALL GENDERS WELCOME!

All. Not *both.*

In that moment, something clicked for me. *All* could mean people other than women and men. That one simple word made space for me, someone who'd always felt a little outside the binary (or sometimes in between). This was a revelation.

Tryouts ended up being challenging and fun. The coach and other skaters were welcoming, and before I knew it, I had officially joined the team. This time, I got asked what type of costume I'd feel comfortable wearing for competitions: a dress or a version with pants.

And when it came time for my teammates to crowd around our coach as she revealed our new costumes, I could finally share everyone's excitement.

Living as my authentic self has made all the difference.

> Not long after I joined the synchro team, I heard the term *nonbinary* for the first time: not relating to, composed of, or involving just two things.

Nonbinary described me perfectly. For years, I'd felt like I had to identify one of only two ways: boy or girl; then man or woman. I didn't understand why none of those words felt right when I was younger. It might have come together much sooner for me if I had met other queer people with similar experiences when I was a child, but as someone who'd grown up in small Midwestern and Southern towns, that wasn't my reality.

Sometimes it makes me sad to think of my younger self, the kid who worked so hard to conform to other people's expectations about their gender. I can imagine growing up in an alternate world where words like *nonbinary* and *queer* and *transgender* were available to me at a much younger age, where specific types of skating costumes, boot colors, and ice-dance steps never hinged on the assumption that I was a girl.

A.J. Sass performs at the 2019 U.S.
Synchronized Skating Championships.

Once I discovered the words to describe my experiences, my world opened up. I felt more confident around friends and at my job, for example. I also realized that much of the anxiety I felt while performing my skating programs melted away now that people could see my true self.

Figure skating has become more inclusive since the 1990s, when I took my first steps onto the ice—and not just by updating the rules and terminology. When I was learning to skate, there were no visible queer athletes in my sport. Adam Rippon was the first out gay figure skater to compete for the United States at the Winter Olympic Games in 2018. Timothy LeDuc, a pairs skater with partner Ashley Cain, became the first nonbinary skater to compete at the Olympics in 2022. While ignorance persists, particularly when it comes to transgender girls and women, it feels like we've taken important strides forward and are moving in the right direction.

Representation is vital to ensure that young skaters feel safe and welcome in sports. It's my hope that in a near future, no young athlete will experience isolation like I felt growing up. Queer kids have just as much of a right to participate in sports as anyone else. They have a right to dress in a way that aligns with their identities and to feel affirmed and supported.

LANDING WITH PRIDE
MY JOURNEY TO THE OLYMPIC PODIUM
BY ADAM RIPPON

When I was nine, I went ice-skating for a classmate's birthday party. What I remember most was seeing all the "real" skaters in the center of the ice. They didn't need to hang on to the wall for balance. They could do jumps and spins. They looked effortless out there.

I wanted to be in the center of the ice.

At age twenty, I went to the 2010 Olympics in Vancouver, Canada, as an alternate. From that moment, I knew I had four years to make the team in 2014. Nothing was going to get in my way. But a lot can change in four years, and being in your twenties is almost as hard as training for the Olympics. I found myself struggling in ways I hadn't before. I was thinking more about the expectations I put on myself, and the pressure that I perceived from people around me.

I wasn't a kid anymore. I was an adult, but I still didn't fully know myself.

Growing up, I was never really sure if I was gay. But I knew, without a doubt, when a boy flirted with me for the first time. It hit me right away, and I didn't want to hide. I needed to share this revelation with those closest to me. That is why, at age twenty-two, I came out to my friends and family. But I wasn't quite ready to share my news with the world.

Figure skating has a complicated relationship with queerness. I had people comment that certain moves I did were too feminine, telling me that I needed to skate in a more masculine way, or to make my programs more masculine.

Looking back, I think some of those people were repeating things they'd been told as kids coming up in the sport. Regardless, it never felt good to hear. I wanted to be the best athlete I could be, and I thought that meant taking advice from everyone around me. Being the perfect skater involved everything I did on and off the ice. If I wanted to win, I needed to play by the rules. It would be best to keep my private life private. The perfect athlete would never risk making people uncomfortable.

The year 2014 felt like a ticking clock on my career—like my last shot at being an Olympian. I was now twenty-four, and time was running out. I wanted to do everything "right."

I didn't want to miss out on this opportunity. I didn't have time to talk about being gay.

There were only two spots for men's single figure skaters on the team, with five or six of us competing for those two spots. In the final competition before the Olympic team would be announced, I needed to skate my absolute best, the best I'd ever skated in my life.

Instead, I skated the *worst* program I've ever done. Under the pressure of "now or never," I crumbled.

To say I was devastated would be a major understatement. I was completely heartbroken. So many people had helped me reach for those Olympics, and I felt like I'd let everyone down when I failed to make the Games. I was a loser. I was a disappointment. Should I retire from skating? What if I just wasn't good enough?

While I was wrestling with those big questions, I kept skating. But I wasn't skating well. I was skating like I didn't know if I wanted to be there. I felt lost. I couldn't help wondering: *What do people think of me? What do* I *think of me?*

When you're at your lowest, sometimes it takes honesty from people who love you to help you out of the dark place. That Thanksgiving in 2014, I went to the house of one of my best friends. I have known her and her family since I was little. Her mom looked at me and said, "You need to pull it together or stop."

It was harsh, but it was exactly what I needed. She woke something inside of me. I decided I *was* going to go for it.

My next event, the national championships, was two months away. If this was the end of my career, I would retire with my head held high. No holding back.

In the past, I had been so afraid of making mistakes that I was getting in my own way. Now I didn't have anything to lose. All that pressure I had felt before was lifted from my shoulders.

Stepping onto the ice at the 2015 national championships, just eight weeks after that Thanksgiving dinner, I skated the best short program I'd done in my career. But I finished fifth. I was frustrated. I'd skated so well and yet I felt the judges were sending me a signal: *Good for you, but it's time to hang it up.*

Before my long program, I reminded myself, *No matter what, the results don't matter. If you skate tomorrow*

and you get fifth, it's going to be the best *fifth place you can be.*

I nailed it. I attacked every element in my long program and finally put it all together when it mattered. It was magical. When the scores came up, the crowd erupted. It was the highest long program score ever recorded at the national championships at the time. The frustration I'd felt the day before was gone. Everything was aligning.

As the last skater took the ice, my first national title looked within reach. But when the scores came in, my fifth-place short program gave just enough room for me to be overtaken in the overall result. I would have to settle for silver.

For one second, I thought, *You've got to be kidding me!* Even though I'd vowed not to be bothered, I was still upset. I couldn't have done any better, and it still wasn't enough.

I stopped myself mid-thought. What was I talking about? The person who'd won deserved to win! And his accomplishment didn't take away from my own. This was the biggest breakthrough moment of my career.

Not winning that competition was one of the best things that has happened to me because I learned that my definition of success was up to me. I did not finish first in that event, but I felt like a champion. No one could take that feeling away.

After that breakout moment in 2015, I decided to do everything *my* way going forward. I didn't need to be a perfect athlete; I could just be the best version of myself. I was going to wear the costumes I wanted, skate to the music I wanted, and be exactly who I wanted to be.

The next big step of my career would be to come out publicly. In the back of my mind, I couldn't shake the fear that being out might change the way I was scored. Ultimately, I thought, if that was true, so be it. It was more important to me to be proudly out than any placement I could ever get.

I figured if I didn't make my coming out a big deal, no one else would, either. After all, so many of my teammates and fellow skaters already knew and supported me. I came out in an article in *Skating* magazine, and it mostly flew under the radar. At that point I was an elite athlete, but I wasn't very well-known. I got a lot of nice notes, and that was it.

I was getting old for figure skating, but I felt stronger than ever. I was out of the closet. I had the right mindset. I felt like I was at the peak of my career.

Sure enough, only a few months after coming out publicly, I clinched my first US national title in January 2016. After the previous two years of disappointment, I felt like I had finally stepped into my light.

I kept skating in an upward trajectory, putting in consistently good programs competition after competition. Even though I'd be twenty-eight for the 2018 Olympics, making that team felt realistic. But this time, I wouldn't put pressure on myself. I would take it step by step.

And then the unthinkable happened. I broke my foot. I'd need to take four months off and miss the 2017 national championships, a critical event on the road to qualifying for the 2018 Games.

A few years earlier, I think this broken foot would have also left me with a broken spirit. But two things had changed: my mindset and my newfound confidence in being an out athlete. I used this recovery time to strengthen my body. I would spend hours in the gym doing every exercise I could think of that didn't involve my foot.

When I could skate again, I got back onto the ice knowing I was all in. If I was going to rank second, or fourth, or sixth, I was going to be the *best* second, fourth, or sixth I'd ever been. It would be amazing to make the Olympic team, but if I

Adam Rippon competes at the Grand Prix of Figure Skating Final in Marseille, France, 2016–17.

didn't qualify, it wouldn't take away from all the things I had already achieved and learned about myself.

In the end, I did make the team for the 2018 Olympics in Pyeongchang, South Korea. I was twenty-eight, one of the oldest skaters to compete, and the oldest first-time Olympian in figure skating since the 1930s.

Eight years and two Games after being an alternate in Vancouver, I was finally an Olympian. When I took the ice in Pyeongchang, I was so confident in all the work I had done leading up to that moment. I was there to skate the very best I could, regardless of all the noise happening outside on social media, and be myself unapologetically.

I won a bronze medal with my team, making me the first openly gay US male athlete to win a medal in a Winter Olympics. It was a moment I will never forget.

Figure skating has grown so much in the last decade. For many years, I was the only out skater. It was a lonely place to be sometimes. But now we're seeing the sport embrace out athletes at every level. The fears that this could affect scores are dissipated by the same mindset that I embraced when I came out: Who cares? Being yourself is more important than anyone's judgment—on or off the ice.

Seeing the figure skating community celebrating Pride Month all over social media and at rinks around the country is surreal and heartening. I am so grateful for the queer athletes who came before me and am so excited for the future generations of figure skaters who will never question whether they can compete as their authentic selves.

Augustus "Gus" Kenworthy

FREESTYLE SKIER

The year 2015 was a big one for athletes coming out. Not only did Adam Rippon come out publicly (page 28), but so did Gus Kenworthy, another athlete in the Winter Olympic Games.

Gus competed for America as a freestyle skier—doing all sorts of twists and flips in the air—in the 2014 Sochi Winter Olympic Games. These Olympics were a big deal. Just before the Games kicked off, Russia, the host nation, passed several antigay propaganda laws.

Some US athletes were warned that they could say whatever they wanted about gay rights on American soil, but once they were in Russia, they had to be careful.

Gus saw the Games as the perfect opportunity to come out and make a big statement in the process. Years later, he told the BBC's *LGBT Sport Podcast* that before the Sochi Games, he had a dream of winning a medal and then kissing his boyfriend on TV, declaring right then and there that he was gay and proud of it.

Gus *did* win a medal. A silver medal in one of the highlights of his illustrious career. But he didn't kiss his boyfriend on TV.

He wasn't ready.

There's no set timeline on coming out. And it's important that people, whether they're famous or not, feel ready whenever they do. No one should be pressured to come out.

And for Gus, it felt like in the world of freestyle skiing, snowboarding, BMX, and similar sports, there was no room to be gay. It felt to him like being gay went against his sport's existing culture. Like he had to choose between his sexuality and the sport he loved so much.

But in October 2015, the silver medalist came out in an *ESPN the Magazine* article, and with three words on Twitter: "I am gay."

And at his next Olympics in 2018, he kissed his boyfriend on TV, making history for LGBTQ+ athletes at the Games.

HOCKEY IS FOR EVERYONE

A CONVERSATION WITH JACK FERNANDES AND IZ FUERTER OF THE NEW YORK CITY GAY HOCKEY ASSOCIATION

You don't often expect to see the word *gay* next to *hockey*. But the New York City Gay Hockey Association has been going strong for over twenty years. An LGBTQ+ sports league based out of New York City, the Gay Hockey Association (GHA) considers it its mission to provide "an environment free of harassment and discrimination for members and friends of the LGBTQ+ community to play ice hockey and fulfill their athletic aspirations," according to its website. And while you don't need to be queer to be a part of the team, the GHA goes out of its way to be a safe space for queer hockey players and fans to love a sport that hasn't always loved them back.

Years of play are not required to join, either—the GHA happily invites players of any experience to join, including beginners. Iz Fuerter (they/them) had always wanted to play hockey but was told when they expressed interest as a kid that "hockey isn't for girls." As an adult, Iz decided to play anyway. They first joined a beginner learning class, where they heard about the GHA. "Some of the other people told me I should look it up, so I did. I emailed right away and said, 'Can I play?' It was the day after registration closed and they were filled for the season. So they told me I could sub, and I did, and from there I got to be on a regular team."

Unlike Iz, Jack Fernandes (he/they) had been playing hockey ever since he was a kid. "I played youth hockey, and I would be the only girl on a team, and then when I was twelve, I played on a girls' travel team, which was super cool. In high school I played on the girls' team for one year, and then on the boys' team another year. And it wasn't always an easy time, like in the locker room. It definitely was not a safe space, but I had to change there anyway, so I didn't really have a choice."

This is one of the reasons Jack says the GHA has been so great for him. "It allows me to keep doing the sport that I love. I don't have to worry about my own safety. I can just go out there and have a great time and be with people like myself. It's everything."

When it comes to the community aspect of the GHA, Iz agrees.

"In the beginners class I started, everyone was really nice, too, but it didn't feel like you could be your full self there. You still had that little barrier of holding back because it was like, I don't know these people outside of two hours on Wednesdays. When I started at GHA, it felt like a real community. The people there had been friends for years, and I was like, okay, this is something I can do for the rest of time."

Without the GHA, Jack doesn't think he'd be able to play hockey at all. "My older brother and my dad play in a league near me in Connecticut, and they've told me that it's not perfect for queer people. There was one time that I went to one of my dad's games, and the boys were hanging afterwards,

A player takes a shot on goal.

and immediately there was overt transphobia. It wasn't even directed towards me. Just in general, they were making transphobic comments."

> "I think it's really important for people to have a safe space. Not only to play hockey. It's mainly hanging out with your friends, and you all just happen to be playing hockey. That's how the GHA feels to me, at least. Especially if your family's not welcoming. I have fifteen people right here who have my back, who are on my team." —IZ FUERTER

Jack agrees with Iz. "It also opens the door for people who didn't feel safe to explore sports as a kid, or who ended up quitting sports after they came out. Now they can get back into it as an adult in a safe space."

The world of hockey has been a tumultuous place for queer players and fans. In 2011, New York Rangers star Sean Avery came out in support of queer marriage. At the time, he was one of only a few athletes in American professional team sports to voice support for gay rights, and there were no active male American players out of the closet. Antigay slurs were also still commonly used during hockey games to insult opponents and officials, and Avery's support for queer marriage caused controversy with both players and fans alike.

While we've come a long way since, the National Hockey League (NHL) still has its flaws when it comes to queer inclusion. In June 2023, the decision was made that, because of a handful of players who didn't want to wear pride jerseys, players would no longer wear special jerseys during warm-ups to mark theme nights, which is when teams show support for a variety of groups. This doesn't just include the LGBTQ+ community but also includes theme nights that support Indigenous groups, the military, and people fighting cancer. Following this decision, the NHL sent a memo announcing the ban also applied to Pride Tape—rainbow-colored tape players wrap around their hockey sticks—saying players weren't allowed to use it at any time.

In a statement, the organization You Can Play, which has worked with the NHL and other sports leagues to help them become more inclusive for members of the LGBTQ+ community, said, "Today's decision means that the over 95% of players who chose to wear a Pride jersey to support the community will now not get an opportunity to do so. The work to make locker rooms, board rooms, and arenas safer, more diverse, and more inclusive needs to be ongoing and purposeful."

Thanks in large part to public backlash and Arizona Coyotes defenseman Travis Dermott defying the ban by using Pride Tape in a game, the NHL rolled back on this rule. "I think they're taking tiny baby steps," Iz says. "And they're working towards the bigger goal, but it still feels like they're letting the transphobic and homophobic fans kind of dictate what they do. Taking away the community nights felt like a really big step backwards. I just don't understand why you wouldn't want to celebrate your fans."

Jack agrees that it all comes down to fans, the people who love hockey. Visibility is important. "You know, the more of us that get involved in sports, the harder it will be for other people to ignore our existence in athletic spaces, and the harder it will be to keep us out. We just have to keep growing it. With the GHA, we have this space in New York, and we're trying to make that space bigger."

That's what it comes down to where the New York City Gay Hockey Association is concerned: being a place for queer hockey lovers to come together and enjoy their sport. The

Members of the New York City Gay Hockey Association playing at Madison Square Garden.

GHA hosts and cosponsors events to increase awareness of ice hockey inclusivity and gay sports in New York, as well as queer health issues. Games are located at Chelsea Piers and are free to attend. Since 2001, its annual Chelsea Challenge has invited LGBTQ+ and LGBTQ+-allied players to compete in a friendly ice hockey tournament.

Queer athletes need places to feel safe and to thrive, to find community, to enjoy their favorite sports just like anyone else, and that's exactly what the GHA does for its members. "GHA is my home away from home," Jack says. "It's my safe space to play the sport that I love."

Want to find out more about the New York City Gay Hockey Association? They invite you to visit their website at nycgha.org.

Courtney Vandersloot and Allie Quigley

TWO WOMEN, A BASKETBALL, AND A DREAM

Growing up in Kent, Washington, Courtney Vandersloot always loved sports. She loved them so much, her dad built her a basketball court right in their backyard. But she rarely used it.

Instead, she'd play on the basketball hoop in front of her neighbor's house, where the boys on the street could see her skills. That way, all of those boys would come out to play with her. And she could show them how much better she was.

Meanwhile, in Joliet, Illinois, young Allie Quigley also loved sports, especially basketball. Her dad did, too, and he was a real athlete. Allie spent a lot of time with him—at the gym, on the court—learning how to play.

He died when she was seven. But Allie and her siblings kept playing in his memory. They kept learning. They kept getting better, and better, and better.

Allie was eleven years old when the Women's National Basketball Association (WNBA) debuted in 1997. It wasn't the first women's professional basketball league, but it was the first to receive full support from the men's league, the National Basketball Association (NBA). Because of this, the very first game—between the New York Liberty and the Los Angeles Sparks—was broadcast on national TV.

That year, Allie spent the entire Christmas season begging for one of the official orange-and-white WNBA basketballs.

Once she had it, she never put the ball down. She just kept working and working on her jump shot. She got very good at that jump shot.

Her family noticed that winning jump shot. They noticed how it looked exactly like her dad's.

Which made Allie want to keep shooting even more.

Back in Washington, Courtney had pictures of Mia Hamm on her bedroom walls. She was dreaming of playing professional soccer.

But when she got to high school, she realized she was most excited to go to basketball practice, to keep working on *those* skills. Somewhere along the line she started dreading soccer practice, too. Her sports dreams started changing.

The summer before her sophomore year, she and a friend road-tripped the four and a half hours to Spokane, Washington, to attend basketball camp at Gonzaga University.

Immediately, Courtney knew that she belonged there. The problem was that at five feet eight, Courtney was on the shorter side for basketball. Which meant she'd have to work extra hard to prove herself to the coaches who watched her play.

So she did.

And those Gonzaga coaches eventually gave her a college scholarship.

Nearly two thousand miles away, Allie found her place at DePaul University in Chicago, Illinois, and in 2008 she was drafted by the WNBA's Seattle Storm.

This marked the start of an unsteady and uncertain four years with the WNBA: In 2008, she played for Phoenix Mercury, and was cut midseason in 2009. In 2010, she played for the San Antonio Silver Stars and the Indiana Fever. In 2011, she signed with Seattle again, where she barely played and was eventually cut again.

Courtney had an excellent senior year at Gonzaga. She was one of the most awarded players of the NCAA that season.

So in 2011, during the WNBA draft, Courtney was selected third out of everyone to sign with the Chicago Sky.

Allie didn't play for the WNBA at all in the 2012 season. She thought her WNBA career was over. Instead, she played overseas, in Slovakia, where she continued working on her jump shots and became one of the EuroLeague's best three-point shooters.

With this boost to her profile, the Chicago Sky signed her the following season. Allie came back to the WNBA after all.

That was how, in 2013, Courtney Vandersloot and Allie Quigley ended up in the same limousine from the same airport, where they had been on the same flight, headed to the same doctor's office for their team physicals.

They talked the entire ride. Courtney, who hated small talk, didn't mind it with Allie. They knew they had feelings for each other right away.

But even though they wanted to be together, they both agreed: Basketball came first. So they waited until the end of that first season before they started dating.

Now partners on and off the basketball court, Courtney and Allie helped bring the Chicago Sky to the WNBA Finals in 2014.

They lost to the Phoenix Mercury. The Chicago Sky didn't win a single game out of three, in a best-out-of-five series. Courtney and Allie didn't let that deter them. They kept working harder.

With their team, and together.

In 2018, they got married. Courtney, who had jammed her ring finger in a basketball game two weeks before the wedding, had to wear her ring on the other hand.

Two years later, Courtney Vandersloot broke the WNBA record for most assists (eighteen!) in a single game.

She broke that record with a pass to her wife, who easily sank the jump shot.

Being teammates and spouses isn't always easy. When they lose, they lose together.

But when they win, they win together, too.

In 2021, the Chicago Sky made it back to the finals against the Phoenix Mercury, again. Courtney Vandersloot and Allie Quigley were the only players still on the team that had played the Mercury in the finals back in 2014.

This time, they won the first game of the five-game series. They lost the second.

But then they won the next *two*.

Which meant the Chicago Sky won the WNBA championship for the first time in franchise history, with Courtney and Allie playing together, side by side.

And they were the first married couple to do so.

Being an athlete means persevering even when it's hard. It means finding the strength and pride to keep going. Growing up, Courtney and Allie each had a lot of reasons to give up, to quit. Courtney could have decided that she was too short to play. Allie could have decided that she didn't want to keep trying after getting cut so many times.

But if they had done that, they wouldn't have gotten to keep playing basketball. They wouldn't have broken records and won a championship.

If they had let all the challenges stop them from going after their dreams, they might never have found each other, either.

THE VISIBILITY OF QUEER WOMEN IN THE WNBA—AND WHAT THAT MEANS TO ME

BY NICOLE MELLEBY

've never felt comfortable in a dress, but I wore them anyway.

There's always been tension between what made me comfortable and how I wanted to look versus what I ended up wearing. For my birthday every year, my mom took me shopping, and I let her pick out dresses and skirts and sweaters that were more her style, more feminine than the types of outfits that caught my eye. Once when I was fourteen, she and I got in a big fight when I came home late from a football game with little time to get ready before my grandparents' big anniversary party. She wanted me to shower and straighten my hair and get into the dress and heels we had picked out. I wanted this, too, if only because my cousins always dressed up and looked so pretty, and I wanted to fit in.

As a teenager, when I needed to choose outfits for a weekend night out, I'd make my best friend pick all my clothes. After graduation, she went to study fashion, while I left high school still not really knowing how to do my own makeup.

When I realized I was a lesbian, but was still in the closet, I started to try even harder to dress the way my mom, my best friend, my cousins— *everyone* it felt like—thought I should. I was afraid of looking "too gay," of giving myself away, of losing hold of this carefully crafted me that I had been presenting as.

Even when I finally did come out, I couldn't let go of that part of me. I couldn't stop trying to look the way I thought I should. I never got any better at doing makeup, but I did learn what dresses looked best on me, how to do my hair so that I looked of a piece next to the other women for group photos at weddings and baby showers and every other event that called for dressing up. Which I thought was fine. Sure, I was more comfortable in pants, but even the queer characters on the TV shows I watched seemed to doll themselves up for a night out.

In the quiet privacy of my bedroom, wearing the comfortable pajama pants I'd bought in the men's section of the department store, I wondered if all these feelings about clothes and identity made me nonbinary, or just a failed woman, or something else entirely.

And then I went to a WNBA game.

I had played sports my entire life—softball, field hockey, and, of course, basketball. I was seven when the WNBA was founded, and slowly throughout the years we shifted from talking only about Michael Jordan and the Chicago Bulls at practices to talking instead about Rebecca Lobo and Becky Hammon and the New York Liberty. I had watched Maya Moore and the Minnesota Lynx win championship after championship, watched Diana Taurasi dominate the court and get a personal foul for kissing Seimone Augustus in the middle of a game.

Somewhere along the line, though, I stopped following. Maybe because women's sports aren't as marketed or readily available as men's, and I didn't exactly feel welcome in men's sport circles. Or maybe because sports stopped playing such a big role in my life after I graduated high school. Whatever the reason, basketball faded from my mind—I forgot about the Bulls hat my dad had brought me home from a work trip in Chicago, I forgot about how often we watched *Space Jam* at sleepovers, I forgot entirely about the WNBA.

While I was visiting a friend in Chicago, we decided to go see the Chicago Sky play.

It was a terrible game. The Sky lost miserably to the Washington Mystics; their shot percentage was less than 30 percent. I didn't really know any of the current players. But we had giant pretzels, and about halfway through the game, my friend pointed to the player taking foul shots to say, "That's Allie Quigley. She's married to Courtney Vandersloot, number twenty-two."

"Wait," I said. "They're wives…on the same *team*?"

Literally and metaphorically, *yes*.

It suddenly didn't matter how badly the Sky had played that day.

What mattered to me were the queer women on the court, living their lives, *married* to each other. I remembered Diana Taurasi's cheeky kiss and personal foul with Seimone Augustus, how she married and had children with her own former teammate Penny Taylor. I remembered Sue Bird coming out in a relationship with Megan Rapinoe. Frankly, I remembered just how queer the WNBA was.

I needed to know more. I started watching every Chicago Sky game I could. I followed them on social media, eagerly scrolling through pictures of the team arriving at the arena all dressed up before games. Yes, some of them were femme—there are WNBA athletes who play in long fake eyelashes and fully done nails—but not all of them. I watched Courtney Vandersloot show up in a button-down shirt and long khaki shorts. I started following other teams and players, watching Minnesota Lynx player Courtney Williams show up with short, shaved hair and a sharp blazer, seeing Phoenix Mercury star Brittney Griner looking unapologetically queer in her tattoos and men's clothes, witnessing Destanni Henderson at the WNBA draft rock a bright teal suit.

I was watching real basketball stars on my TV, most of whom identified as women, dress in a way that made them comfortable, that wasn't maybe conventionally what women wore, that wasn't what the WNBA had expected or wanted them to wear just a few decades before.

It was an authentic representation of queer women like me.

That was when something shifted. When I realized that being uncomfortable in a dress did not make me a failed woman. If anything, I was failing myself by wearing the dresses in the first place, so I stopped.

When I went birthday shopping with my mom that year, I pointed out blazers that I liked. When I had events to dress up for, I picked out a nice pair of pants and a button-down shirt. I started filling my closet with items I felt good in, and donated the ones I didn't. I went to more WNBA games, and I started feeling more comfortable being me by cheering for the players on and off the court.

It's not perfect. *I'm* not perfect. I recently bought a dress to wear to a family wedding. I couldn't figure out what would make me comfortable, because I didn't want to stand out. I didn't want my wardrobe to be a conversation, and a dress felt like the easiest option in the moment. Sometimes I second-guess (or third-guess) an outfit, and sometimes I change my mind before leaving the house.

Maybe it'll be a lifelong journey—maybe how I identify, and the clothes I'm comfortable in, and the way I want to present will shift as I get older. But at least as a WNBA fan, watching these players be unapologetically themselves, I'm starting to be unapologetically myself, too. Witnessing queer athletes makes me a little less lonely.

NICOLE MELLEBY

Nicole Melleby (right) and her wife, Liz Melleby Welch, attending a New York Liberty basketball game.

THE FUNDAMENTALS OF LOSING IN TEAM SPORTS, AND WINNING OREO BLIZZARDS

BY ERIK J. BROWN

When I was six, I wanted to sign up for T-ball because my older brother Sean was playing baseball. I had no idea how terrible I'd be at it.

For those who don't know, the rules for T-ball are similar to those of baseball, but instead of hitting a ball thrown by a six-year-old pitcher, you get to hit the ball off a tee.

And I think they made a new rule, just for me. If you missed off the tee three times in a row, you could walk to first base.

I have terrible hand-eye coordination. Once I realized this, I didn't want to play anymore. But my mom said, "You can't give up on something, you have to see it through." She framed the season as a building block for my future, a way to understand that not everything would be what I expected, and I shouldn't just walk away.

In truth, it was because she had already paid the $350 registration fee and wanted to make sure if she was going to pay that much, I was going to take *something* from the experience. Even if that takeaway was daydreaming and twirling around in right field. Maybe all that daydreaming is what made me a writer today. If so, thanks, Mom! Xoxo.

At the end of the season, we were all given what I *really* took from the experience—a participation trophy! I loved that beautiful, plastic, stone-based prize.

All of those games spent daydreaming finally paid off with this epic award I would put on my dresser. Every day I could wake up, and when I reached for my socks, there it would be. The personification of hard work—specifically my mother's hard work, because it did cost her $350.

On the way home from our award ceremony—held in the prestigious Dairy Queen parking lot—I said to my mom, "I think I want to play again next year."

From the back seat, bewitched by my beautiful trophy, I couldn't hear my mother's knuckles crack as she clenched the steering wheel.

"Are you sure? They don't give those trophies out to everyone in the big-kid league. So you'll only get one if your team wins."

Excuse me? We're expected to *win*? Like, a lot?

I wasn't about that, at all. I was there to daydream out in right field. To sit on the dugout bench and talk Power Rangers and Sega Genesis games with the other kids on the team. Winning was fun, but I didn't want it to be the *goal*. The goal should have been the Oreo Blizzard I had just housed in the Dairy Queen parking lot.

"Okay, never mind," I said, returning to gaze at my prize. That was the end of T-ball.

But I did pick up a new sport. One where I didn't have to worry about my hand-eye coordination because we were only supposed to use our feet in soccer. And our heads—traumatic brain injuries weren't invented yet.

My friend Matt had introduced me to the beautiful game. I mean, I knew what it was, I just didn't know how to play. My brother Sean loved baseball, basketball, and hockey. Soccer was never his thing. So when Matt started teaching me in his backyard, it was something new and exciting. Also my own thing. Something I wasn't just copying off Sean. And it was fun!

Sure, baseball can be fun, but it requires patience. I can watch baseball now and enjoy it, but at the age of nine, my patience was severely lacking.

Soccer offered constant movement and action. Kind of like hockey, but I was scared of falling onto cold ice and breaking something. I was also tall for my age, and my gangly body just couldn't balance correctly on skates, so I'd fall a *lot*. If I fell playing soccer, I landed on grass and just got up again.

Unfortunately, by the time I expressed an interest in soccer, the fall season had already started. So I asked my mom to find me some other option, and that winter, I started playing indoor soccer in a large, heated facility with real turf, where we kicked around a felt-covered soccer ball that looked like a giant tennis ball.

Each Saturday they would divvy us up onto two teams and we'd scrimmage. They kept score, but the teams changed every week, so no one really cared what *team* won, just that they were on the one that did. There were obviously some kids who were better than others, but I was perfectly average. And I was comfortable with that. Because I was having fun.

I continued the indoor league into the spring, and that summer my mom decided to sign me up for soccer camp. Again, I loved it.

So much so that one day I forgot to put on sunblock after lunch, and my super-white skin burned so quickly and so badly that by the time I realized my mistake, my neck was red and I had sun poisoning.

But those little archipelagoes of pus-filled blisters atop my ears were a badge of pride. I had gone to soccer camp, I'd learned a few new tricks, and in the fall of fifth grade, I'd be able to play soccer for the most prestigious organization in Delaware County, Pennsylvania: the Aston Youth Soccer Association.

What I didn't realize, though, was that the coach was the father of George, one of my classmates. So of course, George was the forward. For those who don't know, forwards are the ones who are positioned to score the most goals.

Erik J. Brown in his soccer uniform, 1997.

I didn't care about that. I never wanted to be a forward—and honestly, we were ten years old; it wasn't like we had plays memorized. The basic strategy was to pass it to whoever was open, make sure you kept the ball away from the other team, and take the shot if you were near the goal. But there was another Unspoken Rule that I didn't learn about until after our first doubleheader.

It was a brisk fall Saturday afternoon. We had originally been scheduled for only one game, but the week before there had been a torrential downpour, so the Aston Youth Soccer Association—in its infinite wisdom—decided that the ten-year-olds could just play two games back-to-back.

We lost the first game by just two points. I mean, yes, it was 2–0, but it wasn't like we were completely blown out of the water. No, *that* happened during the second game of the day.

The brisk morning had turned into an annoyingly warm afternoon, and with the sun glaring down at us from the clear blue, breezeless sky it made the second game feel like an eternity. We were tired.

The team we were up against hadn't played a morning game, so they were fresh, warmed up, and ready to basically destroy us. At the time, it felt like we were playing against adult professionals. How were they moving so fast? How did they do that swappy-dribble thing with their feet without kicking their own shins? Why did they have to bounce the ball off one of our faces before kicking it into the goal?

We lost 10–1. And who scored that one goal?

If you guessed me…absolutely not. I just told you I was tired and playing against David Beckham clones dressed as preteens. What makes you think I could score a goal?

If you guessed George? Also, no.

It was the other team who accidentally scored on themselves. And honestly, I think they were just being nice and trying to give us a point.

As soon as the game-ending whistle blew, George lost it. Screaming, crying, and almost throwing up because of his temper tantrum. Then it started to spread like a virus. Other kids on the team were crying; some cursing the God of Soccer, who had forsaken them so; some on their knees ripping out grass with their bare hands—which, this is soccer, sir, use

your cleats—some off to the sidelines, where they stormed past their parents and younger siblings, making beelines for their family minivans to have their meltdowns, which is the appropriate place to melt down, by the way.

All the while leaving me there on the field. Watching the chaos and thinking, *What is wrong with all of you?*

My mom must have seen the look on my face, because afterward, she took me to Dairy Queen for an Oreo Blizzard. This time, she asked if I wanted to keep going, and this time, I said yes. Because I really did like playing soccer. I just didn't like how all the other guys on the team were acting.

The Unspoken Rule, which no one bothered to tell me, was that winning is *everything*. Unbeknownst to me at the time, everyone ages out of playing sports for fun.

This day wasn't *fun* for them. I mean, the second game wasn't fun for me, either. We weren't professional athletes and were bound to get tired after playing two games back-to-back with little training.

What I took from that second loss was the swappy-dribble thing the one kid had perfected. Every time I watched him do it, I thought, *How cool.* He made it look like he was going one way but then would spin the ball around behind him and take it off in a different direction. That was what I was going to practice.

Everyone else just focused on the fact that we lost the game and it was all our fault.

From that day onward, George had to shame us or point out what we were doing wrong. He'd yell at me for not passing the ball to him, or for missing a goal. It was always our fault when things went wrong. And that eventually beat me down, and I'd get in my own head, imagining him freaking out for something I hadn't even done yet. It messed with my confidence.

With every loss, he got madder and madder. And every time he would throw one of his tantrums.

Coach wasn't much better. He'd yell the same stuff from the sidelines or just call out his son's name, directing him around the field. Nepotism, folks.

By the end of the fall, we'd won four whole games. And I decided I wouldn't return for the spring. Adding insult to injury, Dairy Queen was closed for the season.

I didn't play soccer because I wanted to beat other teams. I played soccer because it was fun. Which is where a lot of people fail when it comes to sports.

Before I go any further, I want to clarify that yes, I *love* winning! Everyone loves winning! Winning is the best feeling in the world because it means your skills—what you worked so hard for—were good enough to best the other team.

If you love winning, you have to love losing, too. Not as much, obviously, but you have to acknowledge the loss and learn from it. Losing is how we get better.

When I lost that first doubleheader, I came away with a plan to teach myself how to do the fake-out dribble. The other kids on the team who ran off to have their tantrums kept doing the same things. We never switched up positions or tried to *learn* plays. We just kept hoping we'd get a win.

It was stagnation. We weren't getting better because everyone already thought they were good enough, skill wise, so it must have been that someone else on the team was wrong. My teammates would see a player lose possession of the ball, and it was *that player's* fault because they weren't paying attention. The goalie would let in a goal, and it was *their* fault for not moving fast enough to block it.

All the while, no one was sitting with the loss and saying, "Hey, did you see how Player Eight faked taking the goal but passed instead to Player Thirteen, who got the goal?"

I went on to realize all sports were like that. Everyone wanted to win because winning—especially when you get to the big leagues—equals money. But the big leagues were never in my mind. So I quit.

I stopped playing sports because I wanted the fun part. I wanted to learn a game and get better at it through playing. I was looking to level up and, yeah, maybe win on occasion and get that amazing buzzy feeling under my skin that comes with winning. Especially when it's a close match. But I wouldn't get that again until after college, when I joined a gay rugby team.

I was looking for something outside of work that involved socializing. Most of my hobbies—film, reading, writing—were solitary. Through a friend of a friend, I heard about Philadelphia's gay rugby team and decided to look into it. I had never played rugby, but I had watched games, and it was basically a more exciting version of American football.

And the best part of being on the rugby team was that everyone was there for fun. And they were excited when new people turned up wanting to learn the game that they loved. They separated the newbies during practice to give us one-on-one time, teaching us how to tackle so we wouldn't get knocked out—traumatic brain injuries were finally all the rage. In spare moments during a game, another team member would give pointers, never talking down to us. Instead it was a teammate with more knowledge sharing something they had already learned and perfected. They understood exactly what everyone was there for. To level up and get better at something that brought us joy.

Of course, it was great when we won. But even when we lost, we went out afterward—with the winning team—to eat, talk, have fun, ice our new injuries, and check in on the guy who had gone to the hospital with a dislocated shoulder.

So yes, winning is great. But it's not everything. Everything means winning *and* losing. It's learning from your mistakes, upping your skill level, and getting better. There are lots of ways to do that. But temper tantrums and blaming others will get you nowhere. Helping teammates and sharing knowledge is how you get better.

And remember—whether you win or lose, you always deserve a trophy and an Oreo Blizzard.

Carl Nassib

FIRST OUT GAY ACTIVE PLAYER IN THE NATIONAL FOOTBALL LEAGUE

After growing up playing football in the Philadelphia suburbs, Carl Nassib went on to play for Penn State and then was drafted into the National Football League (NFL) in 2016. Over the course of his career, Carl played seven seasons in the NFL, including for the Tampa Bay Buccaneers, Cleveland Browns, and Las Vegas Raiders, as a defensive lineman. But he's best known for being the first active NFL player to come out.

And he did it on his own terms.

In June 2021, Carl posted a video on Instagram: "I just want to take a quick moment to say that I'm gay. I've been meaning to do this for a while now. But I finally feel comfortable enough to get it off my chest."

He wrote in the post that he'd agonized over this moment for fifteen years. And he was not alone in that pivotal moment. He thanked the league, his team, coaches, and teammates for their support.

That day, jerseys and T-shirts with his name and number were the highest-selling products on the NFL store.

The NFL had existed for 101 years before Carl came out, and yet he was the first player to do so. Six former NFL players came out after they retired, and more were "open secrets" while playing, but Carl was the first to come out while still playing.

Since Carl came out, some college football players have also come out, but no other current NFL players have. While the NFL has made efforts to partner with organizations like The Trevor Project and GLAAD, it's clear that the culture of football continues to make players feel like they must choose between their careers and their sexuality.

Who will be the next change maker on the football field?

CHIPPER'S COMEBACK
GROWING UP TWICE ON THE FOOTBALL FIELD OVER FORTY YEARS AND FOUR QUARTERS

BY KARLEIGH WEBB

PREGAME WARM-UPS—BEGINNINGS

August 1981, Power Park in North Omaha, Nebraska

The 1981 Lil' Vikes Cardinals. Karleigh Webb is in the front row, far left, wearing number "00."

This year, I finally get to play tackle football. I get to wear a helmet and all the pads and everything!

Two weeks ago, I got a phone call from the coach. We were drafted like the pros!

My team is the Cardinals.

Someday I wanna be in the NFL!

My dad says, "You are maybe the littlest person out here, so you have to be the most aggressive, or the bigger kids will run you over."

I can't let that happen!

Dad says, "If you let them push you around, they'll think you're a girl."

My name is Chipper Webb. I'm ten years old and I'm not scared of nothing.

January 2023, Danbury Sports Dome in Danbury, Connecticut

The 2023 Reapers Women's Football team. Karleigh is in the front row, far left, wearing number "46."

I'm nervous like a little kid.

Am I really doing this?

It's six thirty AM in January. It's dark and cold.

I'm old. I'm trans. I haven't played full-contact

football since high school.

So?

I met this group at a festival last summer. One

of their players said, "You look like you could

play a little bit."

I thought she was kidding.

Two months later, I'm at Reapers Women's Football practice thinking, *Will they accept me?*

My name is Karleigh Webb. I'm fifty-one years old. I'm excited and I'm scared.

FIRST QUARTER—LEARNING

August 1981, practice at Power Park

Billy's one of our running backs. Last week he ran through me and called me a chicken.

Right now the ball is in his hands.

Steve is lined up in front of him. Coach Doug has Todd in a three-point stance.

I'm behind Todd. We're all squished between two tackling dummies.

"Welcome to the 'Oklahoma drill,' kid."

I'm not gonna let Billy run past me again. Coach Doug barks, "SET HUT! HUT!"

Billy runs toward the line. Steve has Todd blocked. Which way you goin', Billy? Which way, huh?

Billy wants to run me over.

Head up! Eyes up! Project through him!

My eyes close as I make contact. I know I've got him. Chicken, huh?

I get up to teammates whacking me on the helmet. "GREAT HIT, CHIP!"

My boy Edmund, our star player, is screaming, "Chip's a hitter!"

Even Billy says, "Good tackle."

I notice Coach Walt, the head coach, nodding. "Good tackle, Chipper."

Coach knows my name!

February 2023, practice at Danbury Sports Dome

"Wrong angle, Karleigh. You may have some
speed, but so does this league!"
"Karleigh, this play goes through the two
hole, not the four!"
Coach Gary and Coach Peasy have taught me
more about football in the last month than
I've probably learned in years.
"We are eons away from I Right 36 Lead."
The plays now sound like "Twins Pass Z Zip
Drag 3-4 Arrow."
We're in pads now. When we are doing
warm-up sprints at the start of practice,
I scream the happiest scream! I feel happy
and free, like I'm at home.

That is until somebody hits me.

"Karleigh, with your size and speed, we think it's better for the team if you play linebacker and defensive end."

"I'll play wherever you put me, Coach Gary."

I'm in positions I haven't played since I was ten. Back then there were no strictly assigned positions. Now here I am being triple-teamed by three of our toughest players: Ana, Nicole, and Els. Ana drives me back, then Nicole gets her licks in, and then Els gets me at the end of the play.

"C'mon, Karleigh! Fight us off! THAT'S IT, GIRL!" Ana screams.

"This is not my thing! I'm a defensive back, Coach Peasy!"

"Not anymore, Karleigh," Coach Peasy barks. "Use your hands and fire off the ball! The lowest person wins out here!"

If those three aren't beating on me, Bear Smith is. She's a skilled tackle and may be our strongest player. Practice after practice, she and I fight like cats and dogs.

"Get low and use those hands," she coaches constantly.

I'm the inside linebacker. Sam's at quarterback. Tina's at running back.

She gets the handoff with Bear leading. I'm able to dip under Bear and drive right into Tina, pushing her back 3 yards.

"Whoa!" Tina says. "I wasn't ready for that."

The whole team is fired up. "I can't wait to play ball with you!" Sam says.

The team is yelling and screaming. I smile from ear to ear. Just like that tackle on Billy. I'm a girl who hits just like that!

SECOND QUARTER—BELONGING

September 1981, Power Park in North Omaha, Nebraska

We get our game jerseys the night before the first game of the season.

Coach Walt gives each kid a number and says something about them.

The coach's son, Jeff, is our quarterback, and he gets number 12. Quarterbacks always wear number 12.

Edmund is our star running back, so he's number 34, like Walter Payton.

Big Brent gets 77 because the big kids get big numbers, like 77.

Where's my jersey? No one gets cut in this league, but I'm still worried.

"Next is double zero," Coach says. "This number is special. This number is for the person who I think has the most guts on the team."

Coach pauses and asks, "Who is the kid with the loudest voice, who always talks big?"

Everyone screams in unison, "CHIPPER!"

I go up to get my jersey. A cream jersey with deep red and black stripes, just like the St. Louis Cardinals. The number is a black "00."

There is magic in a jersey.

I sleep in my jersey that night for luck.

We play the Broncos in our first game. My first game. Maybe I'll get the ball. I'll make a tackle. I'll do something to help us win. Anything to win!

When my mom tucked me in last night, she gave me a kiss and said, "No matter what happens tomorrow, I am proud of you because you're out there."

March 25, 2023, a school field in Danbury, Connecticut, two weeks before the first game

After practice one day, Sonya, our team facilitator, hands me my home and road jerseys with a smile on her face. I received number 46 with happy tears.
My teammate Poohdah gives me a hug and says, "You got your jersey now. You ready!"

"That's right," Ana agrees. "This year we're
gonna do some damage, sister!"
Sister. Teammate. Reaper. Me.
When I get back home, I can't resist. I must
try them on. They are tight and "hold-proof."
Red and black at home. A slight gray with red
and black for the road.
Jersey magic never fades.

HALFTIME—NERVES
Saturday April 15, 2023, a hotel in Petersburg, Virginia

We end up at the hotel around one thirty AM
after the long drive south. All week, I have
been anxious. We had more practices and a
film session. During the ride down to Virginia,
I studied my playbook on my iPad.
In my mind, I can see myself running the
ball, catching passes, defending, tackling,
and blocking. I want to play well. I want to
show I belong. I want to earn my teammates'
acceptance and their respect.
I strive to be a good sport, but I've never been
a good loser. I don't like to lose at anything.
When you see me compete, that's when the
little kid inside comes out.

8:00 AM, September 4, 1981, Power Park, opening day of the season, Cardinals versus Broncos

When I get to the park, some of the team is already there. I am in my pads and jersey. I can feel my cleats pierce into the grass.

"Hey, Chipper," Edmund says. "You ready?"

"I'm ready," I say with my voice cracking.

My dad is watching us warm up. His eyes on me, and the entire team. My grandfather is there, too.

"Who are we? CARDINALS! Who? CARDINALS! Who? CARDINALS!

"Who are we gonna beat? BRONCOS! Who? BRONCOS! Who? BRONCOS!"

"Chipper, go out on the kickoff team. Find the person with the ball and take them down!"

"YES, COACH!"

THIRD QUARTER—THE "RIGHT NOW" MOMENT
April 15, 2023, Reapers Women's Football at River City Sting, Sutherland, Virginia

Yard lines. Hash marks. Field turf. Opponents
with different-colored uniforms.
I still can't believe I'm here! I am nervous. I am
anxious. I am excited.

I line up in the backfield on my first play.

We're on offense.

I'm the lead blocker for Tina. I get a partial block on their linebacker, and Tina romps for 40 yards.

We are in position.

We're in a huddle. Sam, our quarterback, gets the play and read from her wristband.

"Pro Strong Right 36 Power."

She then looks at me. "You ready, baby girl?"

I smile and nod.

"You're gettin' the ball, kid!"

WHAT?!

On the snap I take the handoff and race behind Tina. We gain 7 yards, and it sets up the next play. Sam fakes the handoff to me, fakes another to Tina, and then pitches the ball to Aniyah. Her 20-yard scamper puts us ahead 7–0.

Next possession. Their ball. First play on defense. I was warned about their quarterbacks. They switch off between two players, and both are shifty and speedy. The tall quarterback, alone in the backfield, sets up maybe 4 yards off the line.

I'm the outside linebacker, with receivers spread out.

Watch the pass! No one gets behind you!
"I'm on eleven," I scream with my kid voice coming out. Now it feels real.

The player I call out goes into motion. Coach Peasy yells, "You have the next receiver, Karleigh!"

My brain is racing.

"Be ready, defense!" Coach Peasy yells again. Their quarterback turns and runs upfield. I make my first tackle for a 1-yard loss.

"That's how you do it, Karleigh!"

September 1981, Power Park, final minutes of game play, Cardinals versus Broncos

Now I'm on the bench, watching us hang on to an 18–14 lead. I've made two tackles in this game!

Coach Walt yells, "They need a touchdown!"

Their quarterback throws a short pass to one of their running backs. He breaks loose for a big gain. Petey, our safetyman, tackles him and gets hurt on the play.

Coach Walt and Coach Doug strategize.

"We need somebody in for Petey. Who hasn't gotten all their plays for the half yet?"

Coach Pete answers, "Chipper."

"Put Webb in now? If they try to pass, they'll

throw to their tall kid," Coach Doug says. "They'll throw it over Chipper's head."

Coach Walt makes the final call. "Webb! Get in at safety! Let nothing behind you, and do your best!"

It's fourth down, and I'm the smallest kid out there. If I was the Broncos I'd throw at me, too.

But Coach believes in me. That means I can believe in me, too.

On the snap, the tall end runs toward the goal line and then cuts inside.

The quarterback throws it. I jumped for the pass, and I got a hand on it!

Incomplete pass!

Our sideline cheers. I can hear my dad, my mom, my cousin cheering for me.

"Chipper, I knew you could do it," Coach Walt says.

I have goose bumps the rest of the night.

That feeling never goes away.

FOURTH QUARTER—THE COMEBACK

April 15, 2023, Reapers versus Sting, first quarter

It is fourth down and 9 yards. They are
not punting.
They do a fake handoff and a quarterback
run, and we all bit on it.
I am racing from the opposite side of the field

in a dead sprint.
I am all set to make the tackle.
Then I slip. I overplayed. She spins away.
I'm red faced as their quarterback races to the
end zone.
"Karleigh, I told you to break down!"
Coach Peasy chews my ear off for that.
If it weren't for the penalty flag on the
field, I'd be even more embarrassed. The
touchdown is called back. Phew!

Second quarter: Reapers 20, Sting 0

Finally! I'm making tackles and runs and
blocks with a smile on my face.
My team is flying, too. Tina scores. Aniyah
scores again.
Twenty seconds left until halftime, and we're
in control.
I'm thinking of a ten-year-old in Nebraska
who first fell in love with the game.
I'm that same ten-year-old falling in love all
over again.

On the snap, the quarterback rolls to her
right. I'm noticing the slot receiver on that
side and keeping an eye on her. Jessica, our
fast safety, is picking her up.

• • •

I am noticing the other slot receiver as well,
but that throw would be a harder one.
I think they'll try for the running lane, but Bear
breaks through off the snap. She is in their
quarterback's face.
The quarterback throws the ball toward the
inside receiver.
It's the same play! Look it in! Look it in!
The pass looks underthrown, so I make a
break for it.
I look it all the way into both hands.
I have the ball in my hands!
RUN!

A Sting player is close to me and gets a hand
on me, but I shrug her off as I make a cut. Bear
and Poohdah have their quarterback blocked.

I do what I did when I was ten in the open
field. I just run!
Nothing else matters. I am far out in front.

I heard the PA announcer say, "There are
no flags!"
I'm scoring a touchdown? YES!
A blur of memories through 60 yards to the
end zone.

Final score: Reapers 42, Sting 6

"The first game ball of the season," Sonya says.
"It goes to Karleigh. You're a Reaper now."
My teammates give me hugs. I am
overwhelmed with happiness, joy, and
a memory.
"Karleigh," Coach Gary says. "Break us down."
All hands are in the middle of this huddle.
As I look through happy tears, I think I see me
at age ten, in that double-zero jersey, with a
big, happy smile.
We showed them we can play like a girl, huh?

MAKING WAVES
CONFESSIONS OF A WATER FITNESS PRODIGY

BY ISAAC FITZSIMONS

I don't mean to brag, but I'm somewhat of a water fitness prodigy, which isn't a phrase one hears very often, especially not about someone in their thirties.

Created in the 1950s, water fitness as we know it really gained momentum in the '70s and '80s, which is perhaps why the words conjure up the image of a smiling grandma splashing about the pool in a floral bathing cap.

Someone once asked whether my aqua spin class was just for old people. And I get why. The only person in the pool at the time was Sue, a great-grandma several months out from a knee replacement. When I told her to ignore any exercise that was too difficult, she shot me a side-eye and said, "You have *no* idea what they made me do in rehab!" *Touché*. Still, my water fitness clients are trusting me with their bodies, a responsibility I take seriously.

I look back on my journey to becoming an author and recognize the roads that I took, and guideposts I followed. But my path to teaching water fitness was more like a stormy voyage through uncharted waters without a compass for navigation.

Let me be clear: I am not a natural athlete. Freshman year in PE, my badminton partner, a Hungarian boy named Frank, ditched me halfway through the first game because of my total inability to hit the shuttlecock. The truth is, for most of my life, movement and pain went hand in hand. Even walking around the mall with my friends for a couple of hours left me with swollen, achy feet the next day.

In addition to having flat feet, in college, I was diagnosed with dyspraxia—also known as developmental coordination disorder. Suddenly, my difficulty tying my shoes, tendency to bump into things, and messy handwriting made sense.

Underneath all this, simmering consistently beneath the surface, was intense gender dysphoria.

Growing up, I was lucky that my gender expression wasn't a big deal to my parents. My mom didn't bat an eyelid when I emerged from the bathroom (my favorite place to make important life decisions) and announced that I wanted to cut my hair short. In all honesty, my reasons had less to do with gender and more with practicality. Second-grade me was tired of spending every weekend washing, straightening, and styling my long, natural hair.

So I cut it off and dedicated Saturday mornings to useful things like teaching myself how to touch type so that I would no longer have to use a spy decoder ring to decipher my chicken scratch. Thank you, Mavis Beacon.

My mom also never wrestled me into dresses. Her one requirement was that my brother and I looked "neat" for important events. Otherwise, I rocked rugby jerseys and Hawaiian shirts every day. My wardrobe and short hair meant that people who didn't know me assumed I was a boy. Not surprisingly, I didn't really mind most of the time, except for when I had to use public restrooms.

And then came puberty. *Cue dramatic music.* I'm not going to lie: Puberty sucked. At night, I'd wish for one of two things to happen. Either that everything would magically fall into place, and I'd finally feel comfortable in my own skin, or that I'd wake up in a boy's body. When neither came true, I couldn't help but feel like my body had betrayed me.

Let's talk a bit about gender dysphoria. IYKYK, but if you don't, here's how I'd describe it. Imagine being forced into the itchiest sweater you own. You know, the one your great-aunt gave you for your birthday, which you keep hidden away in the back of your closet. But it gets worse. That annoying tag that scratches your neck leaving red welts? Yeah, you can't cut it off. Sorry. And no matter how hard you try, when you pull it on, the sleeves of your

shirt always bunch up at the elbows, and there's a permanent wet patch at your stomach, like you get when you've leaned against a damp sink. That's what gender dysphoria feels like for me, except it's not a sweater I can take off, it's my entire body.

———————

As I developed into adulthood, I felt like my body was plotting against me. As a result, I avoided any activity that drew attention to the fact that I even had a body at all. Things like movement. Plus, my body couldn't even do its simplest job right. How could I trust it with sports?

As with most people, my life came to a sudden halt during the COVID-19 pandemic. Unlike most people, I was already an expert at social distancing and being an introvert, so I had no problem staying holed up in my apartment. But when the world started opening back up, I knew I needed to shake off the cobwebs that had settled after months of inactivity, and so I registered for a morning water aerobics class at the nearby aquatic center.

When I stepped through the door, memories from child-hood immediately flooded me: playing with my brother under the mushroom-spray fountain, devouring greasy pizza that tasted oddly of chlorine. In the two decades since I'd last been at the pool, it was like nothing had changed.

Except, this time, I walked into the men's locker room.

I gingerly slipped into the pool, determined to keep up with the group of seasoned seniors who'd probably been doing water aerobics since before I was born. As I struggled to mimic their movements, I couldn't help but wonder if I had mistakenly signed up for an Olympic training session instead.

My first class was Water Exercise with Karla. She taught me not to be afraid of making a splash. Because of social anxiety, my number one goal in life was to go unnoticed. It felt safer to shrink myself than to speak up or act out. But in the water, even the smallest movement makes waves. When Karla said, "Punch," I punched with everything I had, delighting in the explosion of foaming bubbles all around me.

My next instructor was Flee. She changed my perception of what it means to be a fitness instructor. Trust me, we're not all perfectly toned, muscled superhumans who bark orders like drill sergeants. Flee has multiple sclerosis and teaches from her rollator, using her voice and occasional arm movements to demonstrate the exercises. As I thanked Flee for kicking my butt after a particularly challenging class, she suggested I become an instructor myself, saying that I "moved so beautifully." Standing on the pool deck dripping water, my legs quivering like Jell-O from the workout, I laughed off her compliment. Nobody had ever described my movements as beautiful before.

I continued my aquatic journey and soon found myself in deep water, literally. In the diving well, wearing foam belts to keep afloat, it's easy to get carried away with the current. During my first few classes, I spent more time swimming back into place than I did on the actual exercises. But thanks to Teresa, our firecracker of an instructor, who kept us in line with her energy and enthusiasm, I quickly learned how to engage my core, and Deep Water Running became my favorite class.

Teresa ambushed me one day and asked if I'd be interested in teaching. Again, I resisted, convinced I wasn't qualified to lead a group exercise class. But deep down, I was already mentally choreographing routines to songs on my secret water fitness playlist and growing excited by the idea of sharing my passion for this form of movement with others.

A few months later, Teresa invited me to a training, which I attended. After I became certified, an opportunity to teach aqua spin, a pool-based indoor cycling class, opened up. I accepted.

My first class started with a disaster when the microphone I had clipped to my wrist did a belly flop into the pool as I was demonstrating the opening move. Luckily, I had a spare. When class wrapped up, I made sure to jot down my reflections on things to improve. First on the list: Get a new microphone!

If the microphone is my lifeline, the speaker is my time machine, blasting a mix of classic oldies, a sprinkle of country, and guilty pleasures from the '90s and '00s. I can tell I've picked the perfect song when people's faces glow with the pure

Isaac Fitzsimons doing aqua spin, on a stationary bike in the pool.

joy of nostalgia as they move in the water the same way they used to be able to move on land. The last time it happened, it was during "Dancing in the Dark" by Bruce Springsteen (ask your grandparents). I get that feeling because, as someone who hasn't always trusted their own body, the pool is a sanctuary where I don't have to worry about falling. If I do, the water is always there, ready to catch me.

Now, I can't talk about pools without acknowledging the fact that they can be scary places for marginalized people, and I'm not just talking about the fear of drowning.

In the United States, there's a very real, very shameful history of exclusion in public pools, which still impacts our society today. In the past, pools were segregated first by gender and later by race. With the increase in attacks on transgender rights, we're seeing similar discrimination occurring today.

But water fitness has been so beneficial in helping me heal my relationship with my body as a queer person. And it's my goal to break down these barriers and make the pool a safe and welcoming space for all.

So, when I'm asked if water exercise is for old people, I say yes. It is for old people. And young people. For disabled people. And abled people. All bodies. All genders. All races. Water fitness is for everyone.

I'll see you in the pool!

GET TO KNOW

Billie Jean King

TENNIS CHAMPION
BATTLING THE SEXES

Billie Jean King is American royalty in the world of tennis. A former number one player and winner of thirty-nine Grand Slam tournaments across singles, doubles, and mixed doubles, Billie Jean has been at the forefront of the fight for equality in women's sports.

In 1973, she faced off against Bobby Riggs, a male tennis player who was famous not only for his skill as a tennis player but for the derogatory way he spoke about women's sports, especially women's tennis. He challenged Billie Jean to a "Battle of the Sexes" match. Months earlier, he'd won against Margaret Court, another highly accomplished female tennis player, and he was sure he could win against Billie Jean, too.

Billie Jean won the "Battle of the Sexes" in three straight sets in front of a global television audience of 90 million and almost 31,000 people live in the stadium. It was a momentous turning point for women's tennis, showing that women were every bit the athletes that men were.

In 1981, however, Billie Jean faced the biggest challenge of her career. Her secret girlfriend outed her, without her consent, in a lawsuit. And the backlash was immediate, made even worse because Billie Jean was married to a man at the time. Billie Jean lost sponsors and opportunities because of homophobia. Worried that she would lose her whole career—and that all of women's tennis relied on her success—Billie Jean called her relationship with her girlfriend a mistake. She later said she "couldn't find a closet deep enough."

She didn't want to be responsible for women's tennis losing all the ground it had made in the previous ten years.

She thought her tennis career was over. She was thirty-seven years old, which was old for a tennis player. Her knees were starting to bother her. But tennis wasn't done with Billie Jean, and Billie Jean wasn't done with tennis. In 1982, she made a comeback. When her opponents joked about how she was old and they weren't going to break a sweat in the match against her, Billie Jean was even more determined to win. She played and won, and finished the year ranked fourteenth in the world.

Billie Jean's competitive tennis career slowly ended over the next few years, but her love for the sport remained. She became the coach of the US Olympic women's tennis team, guiding the team to gold medals at the 1996 Atlanta Games. She remained the captain of the US Fed Cup (now called the Billie Jean King Cup) team through 2002.

Eventually, Billie Jean fell in love again. This time, she fell in love with her tennis partner, Ilana Kloss. She and her husband divorced, though they remained close, and after thirty-one years together, Billie Jean and Ilana were wed in 2018 in New York.

Though she no longer plays tennis, Billie Jean continues to fight for equality, equity, and inclusion in sports. And not just in tennis! Billie Jean and Ilana are part of the ownership group of Angel City FC, one of the women's soccer league teams in the US, and Billie Jean entered a partnership to create a new professional women's ice hockey league for North America. The league, Professional Women's Hockey League (PWHL), played its first game in January 2024. Billie Jean's advocacy and her legacy make her one of the most powerful voices we have in American sports today.

"There is no place in any sport for discrimination of any kind. I'm proud to support all transgender athletes who simply want the access and opportunity to compete in the sport they love. The global athletic community grows stronger when we welcome and champion all athletes—including LGBTQI+ athletes." —BILLIE JEAN KING

FOR THE LOVE OF THE HORSE, LOVE OF A BODY

HORSE RIDING AND FINDING MY STRENGTH

BY KATHERINE LOCKE

I didn't fall in love with horses because equestrian sports are the only Olympic sports that don't divide athletes by gender. That's not why I fell in love with horses and with riding.

But it doesn't hurt.

My relationship with my own strength, with the idea of myself as an athlete, and with my own body has ranged from healthy to unhealthy. When I was a kid and a teenager, I didn't have the words for nonbinary. I just knew that I didn't feel like I fit in. In school, in gym class, in my body, and sometimes even at the barn.

I looked down at my body, especially as it was changing during puberty, and it felt alien. It felt like my head and my hands and my feet belonged to me, and everything else was baggage that I carried with me—something confusing, something that didn't feel as if it fit. I tried to ignore it.

As I got older, I tried to make it go away through an eating disorder.

But what ultimately brought me back to my own body was not yoga or meditation or therapy or antidepressants—all of which I tried and some of which are absolutely crucial to my happiness and well-being—it was horses.

I can't remember a time when I didn't love horses. I've loved them since I could talk, since I could express my love. Sometimes, horse girls (and I think of "horse girls" as a gender, encompassing *many* genders within it) are born that way. I started riding when I was eight years old, and I've been riding ever since. I won't tell you how many years that makes, but it's a lot of years.

Katherine on their horse, Beenie, in 2002 at their first horse trial.

On a horse, I can't disappear from my body. I can't reject it, the way it exists in this world. Horseback riding requires a unique set of muscles and a lot of balance. Riding makes you hyperaware of your body. That means even *more* aware than you would normally be. For instance, at my riding lesson last week—I still take lessons weekly—I learned that I curve my upper body to the left, and my right ankle isn't as flexible as my left ankle. I know that when I'm nervous, both on and off a horse, I tend to curl my upper body forward, like I'm making myself smaller.

Good riding requires you to sit up tall and straight, using your abdominal muscles to hold yourself up, your latissimus dorsi muscles to pull your shoulders back, your abductor muscles to hold your legs off the horse and keep your own balance, allowing the horse to move freely.

To become a better rider, I had to start working out off the horse, too. My family and I often joked that I didn't need to know where a gym was in my neighborhood or building because I was never going to go there. But now I use a gym, and I lift weights, and I go for runs.

Because it made me a better rider.

I avoided working out before not because I'm lazy, but because it required a level of body awareness that I avoided, and I was afraid of getting *bigger* in my body. I didn't want to add mass to my body, because adding mass often meant adding curves, and curves exacerbated a gender dysphoria I didn't understand for so many years.

But for the benefit of my horse and her own athletic career, I'm working on making myself a better athlete. It turns out that loving horses and wanting to be a better equestrian are stronger motivators than my fear and discomfort with the body I was born into. And through this sport, I've gained a comfort with this body that has always felt like it is *not mine*. Now I know that this is my head, my hands, my feet, yes, all the body parts I liked and trusted before. But now I also own the abdominal muscles I'm building, and the thigh strength that I'm gaining, and the back strength that lets me hold myself up tall and proud in the saddle.

Turns out that loving a sport means you can learn to love yourself, too.

HIGH-JUMP YOUR HEART OUT

BY QUINCE MOUNTAIN

I should go back and review the footage. It's been almost three years, but I still can't bring myself to rewatch the events in the Wisconsin statehouse when legislators heard public testimony about whether and how to exclude trans and gender nonconforming students from participating in school sports.

Going into the meetings in May 2021, I thought I knew what to expect. During the three-and-a-half-hour drive to Madison from my home in the rural Northwoods, I was more focused on my low-key frustration with some of the activists working for trans inclusion. In our organizing meetings online, these good people, a few whom I'd known for years, almost always made derisive quips about sports before expressing that they did want to help defeat any transphobic bills. Again, these were allies, and I was grateful for their solidarity. But the little "I'm the last person who cares about sportsball…" disclaimers still grated me.

These were activists, writers, academics, and other trans-affirming folks. Some did this advocacy work full-time, and almost all were far more aware of the latest jargon and relevant events than I was. I was there as a trans man but also, as far as I knew, as the only trans Wisconsinite present who made my living in the sports world. I'm a sled dog musher who, at the time, was training for a human-powered endurance race, and I also do wilderness survival challenges. I was the first openly trans competitor in Alaska's famous Iditarod race.

The sports I participate in mostly don't care about gender, at least not explicitly. I was assigned female at birth. And then I was reassigned female over and over, in all the scenarios that continue to happen for young people. I tried my best to *be* female, too. In many ways, I was very comfortable around women. Probably no one in my family or congregation or school ever wanted me to be a woman as much as I wanted that for myself.

But over time and trial, I came to realize that gender wasn't about who I wanted to be. It was just about who I am.

And, aside from having a lot of life experience in girls' and women's spaces, I've always been a pretty basic dude. This isn't a label or an aesthetic choice; it's just how I feel most myself.

Quince Mountain mushing sled dogs.   <small>BLAIR BRAVERMAN</small>

That said, organized team sports for me, as a kid, was not a very welcoming space. I was a skateboarder and played other games with kids on the street or at the park, groups full of boys and sometimes a handful of girls, which was always just fine. But girls' team sports got *real* awkward for me in high school. We didn't have the language for it back then, but my most generous read now is that the girls knew I wasn't like them, and I knew I wasn't like them, and, well, it just was awkward. At the time, there wasn't space for me to play the sports I was best at.

It's important for trans young people to be able to imagine a future. What do *you* want, not just here and now, but in your future? Ignore what you think is possible. Focus on what you want, even years down the road. What do you want to wear to work? Or do you first want to go to college? Do you want to have a lot of friends or just a few close friends? How do you want to do your hair? Do you want to have a partner or partners, romantically or otherwise? Do you want to have kids in your life? Do you want your own apartment, or would you like to live with friends? Maybe you want to live in a tent in the Arctic and do scientific research.

For those of you having a rough time in school or among peers right now, think about the self you want to be in ten years. Imagine telling the story of the lousy time you're having now. How and why each day was a struggle, but you got through it by imagining that one day, you'd be far away from that struggle.

That day will come. It's written into the pages of this book.

When you listen to accomplished athletes discuss their habits, you'll often hear about how they go over plays that happened or they imagine what certain moments could look like. Whether the athlete is a gymnast working out their next floor routine or a baseball player at bat, they imagine what it's like to stick the landing, to block the shot, to kick the game-winning field goal, to steal the base, to swim farther than they've ever swum before, to flip their body through the air and then slice into the water with hardly a splash.

These accomplishments would rarely if ever happen if athletes weren't able to imagine themselves at their very best. You don't hit balls out of the park by imagining, over and over, that you're whiffing.

This is part of the reason sports are sacred, for so many of us. Sports are a great teacher for teamwork, timeliness, and confidence.

A few years ago, I used to worry about the notes from parents. Every week, I'd get notes that said, "Thank you for showing my trans kid that they can grow up and be a successful adult." I'd think, *The kids already know. This note is about the adults, who don't always know what to imagine for their trans kids. Being a successful openly trans person that adults can relate to reassures them that their kids have a future.* I used to worry far more about parents being supportive than about trans and nonbinary kids finding their way to their futures.

Now, in this Wisconsin courthouse, I wasn't so sure. Most of the adults in the room—on both sides "of the issue"—were arguing about whether trans girls would inevitably beat cis girls in competitions. They spent what felt like twenty minutes arguing over high jump competition scores in Oklahoma. As if that were relevant to why any kid wants to play sports.

The adults who supported us were arguing, "No, the trans girls won't win. Don't worry. They won't take anything away from the cis girls." Those against us were saying that we were dangerous, that we didn't belong, that we were either delusional or that we were just trying to get unfair advantages in competition.

The meeting should've ended after an adult used cruel language referring to a trans kid who had told her story about how important it was for her to be able to participate in activities at school.

Trans kids shouldn't have to lead the way. And when the adults in their lives create an explicitly hostile environment, young people don't have a whole lot of power to change things, even if they know what's best for themselves.

But in this statehouse, I was an adult. And I knew I could change the environment, even if it was for just one other person.

This was where I stood up to say that I *hoped* a trans girl won the championship. That it would be amazing.

Because trans kids don't have it easier than cis kids. Trans and nonbinary people are not looking for special treatment. They are just looking to be human and to be a part of things.

And, for what it's worth, it's not only *you* who loses out when you are a trans person who isn't allowed to play with your peers. It's the whole team who loses out on a friend and teammate.

It's unfair that the way things are now, you have to go out of your way to demonstrate that you are not out to harm cisgender, heterosexual families. That you aren't trying to steal others' victories, that you aren't trying to hurt cis kids, that you aren't just looking for attention, that you aren't wrong or delusional about who you are. But, my friends, you do not have to  diminish yourselves in sports or in life to make cis people feel better. I promise you, the people who resent our presence are going to resent us regardless of our performance. So, please, high-jump your beautiful, gender-variant heart out.

I can't wait to watch.

THE WORD SAILOR IS AGENDER

COMPETING AS JUST ME

BY EM DICKSON

've been racing sailboats since before I could walk.

Well, I was in the boats, at least, even if I wasn't holding on to the tiller. My parents didn't let a thing like nap time keep them from their weekly series—they would just stick us up under the cuddy to sleep while they raced.

Suffice it to say, I've been in boats since babyhood, and I've competed in hundreds more races than I could ever count, in all kinds of different sailboats: everything from speed demons like the VX One to a glorified bathtub like the Optimist (Opti). Beetle Cats, fourteen-foot Arey's Pond Catboats, 420s, Lightnings, Lasers, Baybirds, O'Day Day Sailers—the list goes on.

I officially started at sailing school the summer I was eight years old. Sailing school separates kids by experience level rather than age (though age often factors into experience), but

em dickson sailing as a child in 2006.

there is no segregation of gender. My experience at school during PE and in recreational sports leagues was very different. Gender was a constant presence.

In lower school, I was often "one of the boys" when it came to athletic ability, but slotted in with the girls whenever we were separated by gender. I never really felt like I belonged in either space, without knowing why. I had never heard of the word *nonbinary*. What I did hear were things like, "Wow, em's the best girl at this game!"—when I might have been the best in the class at it, regardless of gender.

When I was little, I liked wearing dresses because they were easy (just one article of clothing!), until I became aware that when people saw *dress*, they saw *girl*. At that point, I majorly course corrected by wearing my younger brother's clothes whenever I could get away with it. I didn't have the words for these squirmy feelings. When I was with the boys, I was too much of a girl, and when I was with the girls, I was not quite enough. I didn't know what that made me.

I attended the same school from pre-K through twelfth grade, and I could tell you stories from just about every grade, but I have a lot of gender-related memories from fourth grade in particular. I was the only "girl" in my teacher's bad-handwriting club. And there was what you might call a "recess incident."

The boys in my class were in a football phase, and they decided to ban all the girls from playing, supposedly because "we didn't know how" and would "ruin the game." Eventually they relented, but only to the point of allowing in me plus one girl in our class, since we *did* know how to play. But ten-year-old em was not having it. We'd all been going to school together since kindergarten, playing at recess together for years. This was so unfair.

So, I rallied all the girls in our class and, with the help of the girl who also knew the game, spent several recesses teaching them how to play football. I remember standing in a circle with everyone, practicing throwing and catching the ball while going over the rules together. Finally, after a few lessons, we stated our case to the boys as well as our teacher, and we played in our first football game as a whole class. I'll never forget when one of the least athletic girls outran all the boys for a touchdown, squealing in shocked delight as she threw the ball down in the end zone. I was so proud.

We trickled in and out of football at recess after that first game—maybe playing World Cup or four square instead. But we never had to fight to be "allowed" again. If we wanted to play football, we played. But that wasn't quite the end for me.

I still had those icky feelings inside. Often it was a mix of pride and shame: pride that I was good enough to be "one of the boys," shame that I wasn't *quite* good enough of a girl. Just always this mixture that churned around like a hurricane. Because being a girl in boys' spaces got me attention, even if it wasn't always positive.

Fourth grade was also the first year my younger brother played baseball in a league. We'd grown up playing baseball at summer camps, and we'd created our own one-versus-one version to play at home (though we called it "cricket"), but this was the first time one of us was on a team. Though I wasn't on the roster, I went to just about every practice with my glove and joined in.

My dad always coached our sports teams outside of school, and baseball was no exception. This was also the same recreational league where Dad coached us in soccer and basketball. The next year, I begged him to convince the league to let me join my brother's baseball team. I don't how Dad convinced them, especially since it was more of a conservative Christian league. But he did it, and I got to play baseball with my brother for three seasons, when I was in fifth, sixth, and seventh grades.

I was a pitcher, a center fielder, and a shortstop. Three leadership positions on a baseball diamond. If there had been a vote for team captain, I probably would've won. I wasn't merely good *for a girl*. I didn't need to come with a disclaimer. I was just *good*.

But there was still that mix of pride and shame, from receiving messaging like, "Girls can't play baseball, but it's okay if *you* do." Separating me from both the boys *and* the girls, without actually giving me a place to land. Too much of a girl over here, not enough of a girl over there.

My gender was essentially *tomboy*—a label that only ever seems to be given to sporty white girls. But tomboy as a gender has an expiration date, and that expiration date is puberty. There are no teenage tomboys—at least not past age thirteen or fourteen.

I hit puberty in eighth grade. And that spring, when we went to sign up for our soccer and baseball teams as usual, the league told me to go play softball. Because *girls* play softball.

But I wasn't a softball player. I was a *baseball player. A League of Their Own* had been one of my favorite movies for years by that point—I *knew* girls played baseball. I'd played three years of baseball! I cried, and begged, and pleaded. My parents had several phone calls with the league. I cried and pleaded some more. The league didn't budge.

My dad and brother were already committed for that season, with most of the prior year's teammates still on our roster along with a couple of their dads as assistant coaches. This was my team. These were my teammates. So I brought my beat-up glove and went to every practice. On game days, I warmed up with them in the infield and outfield. And when it came time for the game to begin, I watched from the dugout. I chewed some green-apple-flavored Big League Chew and spit the shells of sunflower seeds out at my feet. I cheered on my team. But my glove stayed on the bench. And I remained on the sidelines.

This time, I'd gotten the wrong kind of attention. Being a "girl" got me kicked out of the league once my body became too obvious to ignore. Too much of an inconvenience. This time, I'd been noticed for the wrong reasons. I was fourteen years old. I just wanted to play baseball. It wasn't my fault I was starting to grow up. Growing up should've had nothing to do with it.

My older sister graduated high school the next year, and we left the league after that. I'd played on over forty teams, across three different sports, often two or more teams a season, from the ages of five to fifteen. My dad had coached over one hundred teams. It wasn't enough.

I don't know what I would've done if sailing hadn't been there for me to fall back on that summer.

As a sailor, I compete in "one design racing," which means all the boats in a race are of the same make and model. I also race dinghies, which are small boats—generally under twenty feet in length—and meant for one, two, or three people. At my sailing school, you spend your first couple of years in "crew class," where each day, you are placed with one teenage instructor and maybe two other kids in a twelve-foot wooden catboat called a Beetle Cat. (Beetle Cats are a classic New England sailboat, first sailed in 1921 and still sailed today.) You learn concepts like "tiller towards trouble"—pushing the steering toward what you want to avoid in order to turn away from it. You might play games like capture the flag, where the flag is a small anchored buoy and you get people out by hitting their sail with a tennis ball. You learn how to sail a course, how to round a mark, how to tie knots, how to safely capsize.

Eventually, you try different kinds of boats—you might move up to Optis, and then 420s, for example. Or you might try Sunfish or Lasers. But the boat you're in is dependent on experience and comfort level. Not your gender.

I can't speak for every sailing or yacht club, though I do believe this is true in most: Gender is incidental.

In sailing, I have never had to think about my gender. It never even came up. And I don't think I ever realized just how much a relief that was until years later.

There's generally no separation by age, either. Sure, certain classes of boats, like Optis, are specifically for youth sailors. And there are regattas that, in addition to presenting awards for the overall results, have awards with specific parameters separated by age category or gender. But those are *additional* awards, not the main award. There are also sportsmanship awards, and at national championships, often an award for the oldest boat—as well as the oldest skipper. I've also seen awards for the biggest age difference between skipper (the person who steers) and crew!

When you're competing in a weather-dependent sport, gender and age are much less of a factor than experience and size. If there's light wind, then you'll benefit from having smaller people in the boat. But if there's heavy wind, and you have those same people in the same boat, you might have trouble keeping the boat flat, which means you'll end up covering more ground and taking longer to go around the course.

Sailing is all about geometry, about finding the fastest way from point A to point B—reading the wind, checking the angles, and, if you don't have right of way, making sure you don't commit a foul; if you do, you'll have to spin (either a 360 or a 720), which takes up precious time. In sailing, every second counts. Gender and age? Not so much.

If you were to visit my clubhouse this summer, you'd find the same crowd there's always been: toddlers racing with their grandparents, against teenagers who are racing against their own parents as well as friends. There aren't *quite* as many ninety-year-olds as nine-year-olds, but there are still active sailors born in just about every one of the last ten decades. In fifty years, if I'm not out on the water, you might find me at the end of the dock, helping to run the races as a Dock Committee member—like my grandmother did before me.

Sailing is a worldwide sport. A competitive sport. A more physically and mentally demanding sport than any of the many others I've competed in. I've been lucky enough to sail in some amazing regattas, like the US Sailing Championship of Champions—the first time at age fourteen and the second at age twenty. I've raced against Olympians and North American champions, some of whom are my relatives.

Where everything else growing up was gendered, sailing was agender. *Sailor* is an agender word. Out on Pleasant Bay, the breeze blowing and the spindrift spraying in my face, I can breathe. There's space for me there. I'm not a girl, or a boy, or too much of one and not enough of the other. I'm just me. em.

And that's how I like it.

SKATING BETWEEN GENDERS ON MY LONGBOARD

BY VINCENT TIRADO

It's the end of a very warm day in May. I'm sweating a little but still enjoying the nice weather after a long, harsh winter. More specifically, I'm glad that all the snow has melted, because it means I can finally get out my longboard and cruise through the streets of the Bronx. I like to throw down my board, jump on, and kick leisurely, feeling the wind in my hair as I go. When there's enough momentum, the experience is a little like flying. There's a weightlessness to it. For a moment, gravity doesn't seem to exist. Instead, I'm gliding through the world like a bird.

My board doesn't even feel like an external object—it feels like a part of me. An extension of my will. And at the same time, my longboard has its attitude. I've never been the kind of person to name my longboard, but if I were, I'd probably call it Rio, Spanish for river. The way it rolls over concrete and stone is as fluid as water.

Going up a hill, however, is still a bit of an exercise. I have to kick harder. The steeper the hill, the deeper the strain in my legs. It's a temporary pain that doesn't faze me so much. Even before longboarding, I enjoyed various forms of exercise, going from the volleyball team in middle school to the cross-country team in high school.

At the top of the hill at Bill Rainey Park, I give one last kick before riding down on the other side. My weight does most of the work, and all I have to do is lean to one side or another to turn the way I need to. I almost feel like a bird of prey, diving low to the ground for a kill. I have to be precise as I cut around people and sometimes even cars. I'm more attentive. A little panicked if I'm coming up against a crowd of people.

And every abnormally large crack and rock brings another mental calculation over whether I can safely go over it, or if I should dismount or go around.

If you've never seen a longboard, it is very similar to a skateboard. But the board is longer, the wheels are larger and more shock absorbent, and the trucks that connect the wheels to the board are more flexible to accommodate for the turns. It's also much faster than a regular skateboard, making it an enticing method of transportation for people who want to travel quickly without bus fare or a car.

At this point, I've been longboarding for a few months, using it as my main method of transportation from my grandmother's house, where I live, to my mother's house, and to my after-school job and back. I'm about to enter senior year of high school.

I have a number of friends who also longboard, but they take their cruising to the next level and bomb hills—that's when you skate down a very steep hill very quickly. If you're not careful, the end result can be...messy. None of us wear helmets, or even kneepads and elbow pads, which makes the entire thing very dangerous.

But I don't bomb hills. I don't like doing anything that's tempting fate, and the idea of riding so fast that I can't easily stop without taking a nasty fall makes my heart want to skip town. I've fallen off my board before and gotten very good at self-applying first aid, but I wouldn't want to risk a fracture.

Instead, I cruise. And on this day, I'm cruising to the top of a short hill at the park. The park is filled with people—mostly older men and a few small kids who might be theirs. They gather around the part of the park that meets the baseball field, watching teams warm up before a game. It feels like an average day in the Bronx—until a little boy stops me.

He barely comes up to my hip, and he's hesitant, or maybe just very shy, but he stops me anyway.

"Excuse me," he asks. "Are you a girl or a boy?"

The question takes me by surprise. It's the first time someone has ever asked. I am a teen girl, wearing my school uniform complete with a uniform *skirt* with built-in shorts. But I have short hair—nearly a buzz cut—and I am on my longboard, both "boy" things.

I don't remember if I felt eyes on me at the moment—maybe someone put this child up to asking me this question. Regardless, I wasn't offended by it. Strangely enough, I was ecstatic. The question filled me with glee.

Thinking back to it now, I think it was the first time I experienced gender euphoria.

Gender euphoria is generally described as feeling joy or satisfaction in your gender identity. Most people who don't have to think twice about the way they are perceived experience gender euphoria. They feel "right" in their gender. They're at home with it, comfortable and secure. On the flip side, there's gender dysphoria, where your assigned gender causes distress.

Up until that moment, I wasn't particularly distressed—but I also wasn't satisfied. I didn't feel at home as a girl, and it felt like a lot of my hobbies at the time reflected that. I liked video games and longboarding. I had very little interest in feminine clothes or accessories.

But I also didn't quite feel like a boy, either. If I thought about *being* a boy, it caused me more acute distress than the idea of being a girl—but that didn't mean I was happy being a girl. On a good day, I was indifferent to the idea of girlhood. On a bad day, it was like wearing a too-large shirt. Ill fitting but doable.

There were very few times when I didn't feel like I was just acting the part of a girl. Usually whenever I played sports. I was on the cross-country team, the soccer team, and the track-and-field team in high school. Even outside of school, I'd make time to go to the gym and work on my endurance.

Any form of exercise felt good to me, and not just because of the rush of endorphins. It helped bring me out of my own head. I was more present and felt deeply satisfied whenever I pushed my limits. And best of all, exercise helped me sleep better at night.

Exercise never felt exclusively like a "boy" hobby. It was something I could do simply by virtue of having a body. And I loved to see what my body could do.

Despite not knowing a single other girl with a longboard, longboarding never felt exclusively for the boys. For me, it just felt *right*. It made sense. If I could ride across my neighborhood in half the time it would've taken if I walked, why wouldn't I?

I could tell whenever people did a double take, when their eyes were glued to me a second longer as I passed by. Sometimes strangers shouted words of encouragement. It was interesting—to know that I could garner attention just by doing something that girls "shouldn't" do. The verbal shouts of approval came with the silent acknowledgment of this expectation. *Girls can do anything that boys can do, so good for you for actually trying* seemed to be the subtext of these interactions.

It made me uncomfortable. And it made me feel pressured. No one said it out loud, but I could tell that people expected me to be as good as a boy; otherwise the hobby was wasted on me. If I fell, it would be more proof that I should stop.

But I wouldn't stop. When I went longboarding, whether in skirts or pants, I'd ignore gawkers and focus on the ride.

skateboard

longboard

I just didn't imagine that I would shatter the expectation so much that it might confuse a child. I had to wonder—were there more people who couldn't tell I was a girl? Were the quiet pedestrians who said nothing while I cruised around just confident that I was a boy?

And if so, how much could I get away with if people thought I was a boy?

All of these questions made me think back to the reason I got into longboarding.

In the Bronx, there are many skate parks a person can enjoy. There's the Bronx Skate Park, the River Avenue Skate Park, the Van Cortlandt Skate Park, the Playground 134 Skate Park, and more. Even so, skateboarding remains a subculture. Skateboarding seemed cool, countercultural, and almost impenetrable. There was a bond between skaters. Shared experiences and passion brought them close. And it seemed like unless you had those same experiences of falling off your board, scraping knees, and spraining limbs—and remained passionate enough to keep going despite the pain—you could not be included in that bond.

And there were hardly any girls at any of these skate parks. I knew of some girls who would hang out with the boys and try their skateboards, but they never really got into it. I remember trying to skate on a friend's skateboard once, and even I didn't like it. The less-shock-absorbent wheels meant that every time I rolled over a small crack, I'd be in danger of falling. Because the board was smaller, I couldn't spread my legs wider, so I felt unbalanced.

I didn't find out about longboards until someone brought one to school. He was so much faster than the other skaters on this larger board, and his riding was a lot smoother.

I realized then that what I needed wasn't a skateboard—it was a longboard. Unfortunately, I soon found out how expensive a longboard was. With money tight in the house and my mom's adamant disapproval of the hobby, I would have to come up with the cash myself.

I spent months saving up birthday money and paychecks from my after-school job to be able to afford my first longboard. Even then, the Bronx didn't have a skate shop, so I needed to travel all the way to Brooklyn, to the Longboard Loft, a shop that specialized in longboards.

The trip took about an hour, which was plenty of time for my friend Luis to ask me questions about what I wanted my board to be able to do—as well as my budget. Longboards are expensive and can run well into the hundreds if you aren't intentional about every aspect of your board. And I was getting a custom-built board. That meant I was picking out the wheels, the trunk, and the board itself for the clerk to put together.

I remember choosing a Bustin board, one of many long-board brands. It was about thirty-nine inches long with a loose trunk so I could cruise through the Bronx and easily turn corners. Once it was put together, they allowed me to test it out in the shop. I stood on the board and pressed my full weight into it. It was sturdier than I imagined and stronger than I expected. And it was mine. I was excited. I was terrified. Anxiety looped back to excitement and vice versa. My nerves were shaking so hard, I almost couldn't differentiate between the two. But once I shelled out the cash, it was hard to take it back.

Before we went home, Luis had to teach me how to take care of my board. It wasn't enough that I just ride it. I had to know how to keep it properly cleaned as well. If too much grime built up in the wheels, it would impact the quality of a good ride or damage the parts. At worse, it could cause an accident. So I had to buy a T-tool, a metal tool for maintaining and adjusting a longboard. Luis showed me how to take it apart, to remove the nuts and bearings to make it easier to clean.

The relationship between the board and the boarder became more intimate in this moment. This wasn't just a method of transportation anymore. It was a responsibility. I could feel myself growing attached to my board before we even left the shop.

"And," he said, "if for some reason, your board snaps in two, you can still take off the trunk and wheels to put on the next one."

He didn't know it, but it meant a lot to me that Luis believed in me enough to show me how to take care of my board and reuse the parts. It was like he was saying, *I know you won't give up.*

Funnily enough, I was never fearful of not being seen as "girly." I didn't care about being feminine, but everyone else deemed it important, so I went along with it when I could. I kept my hair long and straightened up until the start of that same junior year.

That year was also the start of a new movement that was spreading through the community—the natural hair movement. It was the start of when so many Black women decided to do away with chemically relaxed hair and revert back to how their hair naturally grew—whether curly, coily, or kinky. Many Black women I knew did the "big chop," including my best friend. They cut off all their hair to make room for the new growth. It gave me the courage I needed to do the same. I was tired of going to Dominican salons week after week to straighten the new growth from my scalp. It definitely wasn't healthy and was going to make me go bald if I kept it up.

Often with the big chop, Black women were concerned they wouldn't look feminine enough. For them, femininity is a higher hurdle to jump. Makeup is often a must, nails have to be perfectly manicured, outfits must be flattering.

None of that appealed to me. I never wore makeup, and I didn't mind if I looked less like a girl with short hair. Instead, I welcomed it.

I would simply be a girl who just happened to have short hair, or a girl who just happened to enjoy longboarding. It didn't make sense to me that girlhood came with a checklist, a set of expectations that I had to meet to continue subscribing to the gender. Sure, most girls maybe didn't keep short hair—but I did. Most girls didn't longboard, either—I still did. Maybe I was the exception, and not the rule. Maybe I was even the rule breaker. But at the end of the day, I was still me.

And though I didn't go to the skate parks, I still hung out with those few guy friends who longboarded. When they weren't bombing hills, they would invite me to go on long trips from the start of Hunts Point in the Bronx all the way to the end of Manhattan, right before the ferry. Those guys were good friends to me. They were respectful enough of our physical differences that they didn't roughhouse with me like they did with one another on occasion, but they didn't treat me delicately, either. I think that's what helped me feel secure enough to keep longboarding. We had our own kind of unique friendship—our own kind of bond that made me feel supported in my interest. I sort of understood skateboarders, in that respect. It's nice to be part of a supportive community, where people won't mock you if you do happen to fall and hurt yourself. There is nothing worse than hearing "I told you so" when making a mistake.

In hindsight, I do wish more girls had picked up longboarding. I remember a few girls who had shown interest but held back, maybe out of fear of falling and proving all those other people right. I don't blame them. Expectations are hard to break away from.

However, I do think it gets easier. Years later, after I had bought a new longboard, my mother told me that my younger cousin wanted to learn how to skate. I decided to give her my old longboard and impart the same wisdom that Luis had given to me. I don't know if she stuck with it. At the time, I was a busy college student and only longboarded between classes on campus. Still, I hoped she would discover the joy of cruising. I wanted more girls to experience gliding through the streets.

Though I didn't stop rolling when that young boy approached, I did give him an answer. The question, both perplexing me and delighting me, made me realize that I didn't have to choose girl or boy. Those were not my only options.

I laughed as I replied, "Who knows?"

Maybe it would have been better if I'd just said, *Girl*, and let him live in the possibility that girls could have the same interests as boys. It seems obvious now, but oddly enough, that's a lesson children have to learn time and time again. There are always people who will want to separate boys and girls based on what they "should" and "shouldn't" do. Kids are smart enough to notice the differences in expectations. And when they do, they internalize them.

When that little boy asked me if I was a boy or a girl, I realized I didn't have to be a boy to enjoy longboarding, and I didn't have to be a girl to prove a point about who's "allowed" to do longboarding. I was just me, and that was enough to make people curious about who I was and what I was doing.

These days, I don't longboard anymore, and I'm no longer a girl. I'm nonbinary. But I still love exercise and have begun lifting weights. Sometimes, I think about whether I'd like to pursue bodybuilding. Even though bodybuilding is similar to longboarding—a male-dominated field that women aren't expected to enter—I don't feel as self-conscious when I consider it. I'm even more androgynous now than when that boy first stopped me in the park. When people look at me, they don't pause as long. I assume it's because they've decided on their own what my gender must be.

I'm sure that they're wrong, and it doesn't bother me. I don't owe anyone an answer for why I enjoy my sports or hobbies.

A fixed gender identity is not a prerequisite for being yourself.

Ellia Green

RUGBY CHAMPION, OLYMPIC GOLD MEDALIST, AND TRANSGENDER ACTIVIST

In 2016, Ellia Green won a gold medal at the Rio de Janeiro Olympics as part of the Australian rugby sevens team. Ellia became the first Olympian to come out as a transgender man in 2022, and now uses he/him and they/them pronouns. Seeing so few trans athletes at the elite level, he decided to come out publicly in the face of World Rugby's decision to bar transgender women from playing the sport.

It was also important to Ellia, who struggled with his own mental health and depression, to draw attention to this serious health issue: Studies say that more than 40 percent of trans youth have considered suicide. In an article in the *Sydney Morning Herald*, Ellia stated, "Banning transgender people from sport is disgraceful and hurtful. It only means the rates of suicide and mental health issues will get even worse."

Ellia retired from rugby in 2021 to transition. His plan had been to participate in the 2020 Tokyo Olympics and then begin his transition. He was heartbroken when he wasn't selected to be on the team, although he now had the surgery to look forward to. About his surgery, Ellia told Outsports, "When I had time on my own, thinking about my surgery and having this next part of my life to look forward to was pure joy, pure happiness, excitement."

Ellia is now proud to be a full-time dad. His biggest hope is that his story will inspire other trans people, especially athletes, to be confident in deciding who they want to be.

"It is possible to live a life as your true self. It is possible to find love, to have babies, to get married, to do all that, even though there are laws out there and people saying you can and can't do that. You can do it." —ELLIA GREEN

MAYBE IT WAS DRAG
FINDING MYSELF AS A SKATER BY PERFORMING AS SOMEONE ELSE

BY KARINA MANTA

Standing inside a sweaty crowd, I gazed toward an empty stage. Two friends and I fidgeted with anticipation. I had never attended a drag show before, and I wasn't quite sure what to expect. Speakers blasted pop songs, and I could see the tops of various heads bobbing up and down to the melodies. The grass beneath us, dry from the summer heat, shimmered with glitter that had been shed from a few elaborate rainbow outfits. The gleaming dust made it seem like the earth was releasing speckles of joy just for us. Just for Pride.

Then the pop music faded, and the stage lights flickered on. The first performer emerged from backstage. Her high-heeled shoes strutted before the crowd. Her dress rippled with wispy feathers. When she began to lip-sync to a Cher song, the audience let out a collective squeal. When she spun around and around onstage—a kaleidoscope of makeup and glitter—I threw my own hands into the air and cheered.

Several performers took the stage that day—a queen with unforgettable red boots, another with a rhinestone cowboy hat, and a final performer who appeared in an infinite rotation of wigs. My friends and I watched performers of all genders, and skin colors, and body types. Every one of them knew how to command an audience.

I left feeling buoyant. The whole car ride home, my friends and I lip-synced like we were auditioning for next year's Pride events. We rolled down the windows, not the least bit worried about the other drivers that might see us while we belted under the red glow of the stoplights. For a few minutes, we were as beautiful, and creative, and free as the queens.

I love drag shows for a lot of the same reasons I love figure skating. I'm a sucker for sparkles and dancing. I love the magic of a spectacle and transforming into a version of myself that's bolder and brighter than the person I am in my day-to-day life.

But there were times, especially when I was younger, when figure skating felt very different from the joy of a drag performance. There were times when standing on ice in front of a crowd felt like the exact opposite of freedom.

I've been skating since I was five years old, but when I was about thirteen, the ice rinks that I had always considered to be my home suddenly grew more hostile.

I was beginning to sense that something inside me didn't mesh with the rigid world of figure skating. I couldn't put my finger on why I felt so different—maybe it was a discomfort with my changing body, maybe it was a growing awareness of the unforgiving nature of the sport, or maybe it was a normal middle school shift in my personality—but the reason didn't seem to matter much. The rink became a lonely place.

As a kid, I relished any opportunity to get creative. My favorite part of skating had always been the artistry. I used to mess around on practice sessions, imagining my own choreography to the background music that played over the speakers, but I had long since abandoned that playfulness. The potential embarrassment felt too high. Instead of experimenting the way I used to, I took careful instructions from my coaches and choreographers, never veering from their prescribed movements.

My head coach, Uyen, a woman I had known for many years, noticed my increased caution, and she attempted to coax me out of that fear. One day during a lesson, after running the entirety of my program, she called me over to the boards.

"Good job," Uyen said. "When you catch your breath, I want to revisit the footwork. I think you can be more expressive with your upper body."

I nodded obediently.

"How do you want me to change my arm movements?" I asked.

"I'm not sure. Why don't you experiment a little?"

I skated away. How was I supposed to experiment? I was confident in my ability to execute jumps and spins, but the thought of freely expressing myself opened a world of doubts. What if I made mistakes? What if my choices just confirmed to audiences that I was weirder than the other skaters? What if my decisions fueled the growing suspicion that loomed in my most tender moments—the suspicion that there was something wrong with me?

As I performed my footwork for the second time, I attempted to add a few gestures with my arms. I stretched my fingertips skyward. I gracefully circled my wrists. But mostly, I blushed and looked down at the ice, embarrassed by my efforts to create something beautiful.

When I returned to my coach, she looked disappointed.

"I think you can take bigger risks," she suggested.

"I'll keep trying," I promised, though my voice wavered as I spoke.

As the weeks carried on, the situation only worsened. My results at the regional championships—an event that I had prepared for all season—were devastating. Not only did I fall on elements I could normally execute in my sleep, but I lost all sense of showmanship. In the middle of the performance, I felt my facial expressions turn robotic and cold. As I took my final bows, I found myself wondering why I bothered with skating anymore, and I continued questioning myself after returning home from the competition. On days when I managed to drag myself to practice sessions, I would skate around in aimless circles, avoiding eye contact with anyone else on the ice.

In an effort to shake me out of my slump, Uyen arrived at the rink one afternoon with a suggestion. She called another one of her skaters over, a bubbly, curly-haired girl named Nikki.

"There's a showcase competition coming up," she mentioned. "It might be fun for you two to compete as a duet."

Showcase competitions were different from the events I typically participated in. While most competitive skating events fall into four strict categories—men's singles, women's singles, pairs, and ice dance—showcase competitions provided a different kind of atmosphere where the categories were more fluid. Boys and girls often competed against one another in the same events, and duet categories allowed skaters of the same gender to partner in their routines, unlike pairs or ice dance, where girls were always required to partner with boys. The main focus of showcase events was not to execute complicated elements or abide by the rigid standards of Olympic skating. Instead, skaters could focus on portraying emotions and demonstrating theatrical skills.

I immediately took to the idea of skating with Nikki. She was one of my closest friends at the rink. She was smiley and beautiful. A former cheerleader. In a lot of ways, I thought she was the epitome of what a skater should be. I might have even thought she was the epitome of what a *girl* should be, and I often wished her ease would rub off on me.

I shrugged at our coach's suggestion and peeked over at Nikki. The idea of doing the showcase event sounded exciting, but I worried Nikki might not share my enthusiasm.

"Yes! We have to skate together!" Nikki said. "It'll be so fun!"

I let myself smile. "Okay. I'm in!"

Uyen looked pleased. She went on to tell us that she didn't want to be the one to choreograph our program. She trusted us to work together to pick a theme and create the whole routine in collaboration.

Over the next few days, I thought of little besides our routine. When I was supposed to be paying attention in class, I was brainstorming. Whenever a song came on over the radio, I imagined how Nikki and I might skate to it. Finally, inspiration struck one afternoon when my brothers and I were playing video games. I was delighted by my new idea, but I wasn't sure if Nikki would be on board. My idea wasn't beautiful or girly. It wasn't the kind of story that skaters usually portrayed in their programs, and it definitely wasn't the kind of thing that would allow me to fly under the radar.

I held my breath and texted her. "What if we skated as Mario and Luigi for our duet?"

I waited anxiously for Nikki's reply. I wondered if I had made a mistake with my suggestion, but to my relief, my phone buzzed just seconds later.

"That's perfect!" she replied. "I'll be Luigi since I'm taller."

"I guess that makes me Mario!" I typed back, exhaling the breath I had been holding in.

The next day, I arrived at the ice rink giddy. I could hardly put my skates on fast enough because I was so eager to get

Nikki (left) and Karina (right) in costume
for their Super Mario Brothers–inspired
performance.

started. Nikki had the same buzzing energy. We got straight
to work.

"Okay, what if we start pressed up against the wall," she
suggested, "like we're two-dimensional!"

"Oh my gosh, yes! What if then we jumped and high-fived
like they do in the video game?"

"I love that! Yes!"

"What if we figure out how to pair spin together? Like the
skaters on TV?"

"What if we slide on our bellies?"

"This is going to be amazing!"

Brainstorming choreography usually made me unbearably nervous, yet I was suddenly full of ideas, and Nikki made me feel like all of my contributions were worthwhile. With Nikki, I wasn't afraid to suggest something that might go against the usual grace and elegance that was expected of us as skaters. As Mario and Luigi, we didn't need to appear feminine and faultless. We could be silly. We could be daring. I could be creative again. Finally.

The program came together in record time. In a matter of days, the routine was complete. We knew we had done a great job, because every time we played our music on practice sessions, the other skaters would pause along the edges of the rink to watch and then erupt into cheers just as Nikki and I slid into our final poses. By the day of the competition, we knew we were ready.

A typical morning of a performance involved a lot of makeup and hairstyling, but this event would be different. Instead of wearing shiny ponytails and gloss-covered lips, we disguised our long hair with caps and glued fake mustaches onto our faces. Instead of slipping into tiny rhinestone dresses, we put on identical pairs of baggy overalls.

When we finally took the ice together, moving with staccato steps like we were made of pixels, the audience laughed and cheered. As our music began to play, I felt at home. For the first time in a very long time, skating was fun again. Nikki and I punched invisible boxes above us. We performed silly dance moves in complete unison. We slid across the ice on our bellies.

When the program ended, and Nikki and I took our final bow together, I even noticed one of the judges smiling. We ended up winning the event, but the results no longer felt important. I was already proud of the program we'd created together. I was so relieved to know that I hadn't entirely lost my love for skating.

At the time, I had never heard of drag performances. I didn't know there was a whole art form dedicated to creative expressions of gender. I didn't know that Nikki and I were dipping our skates into a whole world of comedy, and fashion, and dancing. I didn't know that drag was an art form pioneered by the queer community—a community where I would eventually find belonging.

Years later, I would learn more about my own identity, and I would meet other people who understood the feelings of being an outsider that I had carried for so long, and those people would take me to my first Pride, where I would stand in the crowd at a drag show. And I would feel my heart squeeze with recognition.

Maybe the performance Nikki and I had created was more than a skating routine. Maybe it was drag.

Karina Manta performs with Joe Johnson at the 2018 Skate America international competition.

• • •

Now it's been over ten years since Nikki and I competed together. Our routine helped me rekindle my love for the sport, and I went on to skate for many more years to come—so many, in fact, that I eventually became a professional figure skater.

These days, I've skated all over the world, I've won shiny medals, and I've choreographed programs for millions of people to watch on TV. I still have moments of doubt. Sometimes, I find myself falling back into old habits, wondering if I'll make a mistake or embarrass myself, like I used to worry all those years ago.

But now, when the doubts creep in, I remind myself that figure skating should be fun—it should feel like lip-syncing on a car ride home. When I worry that I don't belong, I remember that my skating has always been more interesting when I let myself expand beyond the strict categories still enforced by the sport. When I feel stifled by the pressure, I remember I have friends like Nikki by my side—friends who will cheer on all my ideas, friends who don't need me to be anyone but myself.

I picture every skating program I create as a little drag performance, and that helps me keep the doubts at bay.

MY WHOLE LIFE AHEAD OF ME
THE END OF MY SWIMMING CAREER

BY SCHUYLER BAILAR

At the edge of the pool, I lean forward and let myself fall in. My body melts into the water, and I swim. "Two thousand yards to warm down," Coach had said. "Even though it's your last race. Warm down."

My last race, I think. *It's over. It's* really *over.*

The tears begin, mixing into the pool. *Thank you, body.* I feel myself exhale.

100 yards. Everything aches, the remnants of the race still holding my muscles tight. I consider stopping at the wall, but I know I should keep going. *Flush it all out*, my middle school coach used to say.

I listen to the water rush past my ears as I push off the wall. "Sink into it," I whisper to myself. I take my strokes slowly, focusing on technique. My right hand enters first. I catch the water with a slight bend in my wrist, then in my elbow, and then I pull all the way through. Left arm. Right arm. Left. Right. I savor the feeling of powering myself through the water.

This competition—this final race—marks the end of eighteen years of competitive swimming—four years in the men's category and fourteen in the women's.

Yesterday, I FaceTimed myself. I set up my phone to record me talking to me. Mostly, I cried, brimming with grief. The impending end of my swim career has been clawing at my chest, demanding I make this final competition count. *Make this one the best one!*

200 yards. I switch from freestyle to breaststroke—my best stroke.

There is no way to sum up eighteen years of swimming in one competition or one race. There is no way to ever thank swimming for all it has given me and all that I've learned.

There is no essay, no short story, no way I could ever convey the complexity of being a mixed-race Korean American queer transgender swimmer.

But in the water, I have nothing to explain.

As the yards go by, my muscles relax, and the tension from the race subsides. *Don't go*, I whisper, wanting to hold on. *Stay, just a little longer.* I know I will never feel quite like this again.

At the wall, I flip, pausing when I'm upside down. I touch my hands to my chest—bare against the water, my mastectomy scar bold, as always—and I exhale. *This is me. All of me.*

300 yards. I push off the wall, and with every stroke, I dive back into old races, remembering how I arrived here.

I feel so lucky for a childhood often spent in the pool and the ocean. I can't recall a time without swimming. No matter what the kids at school said about me or my gender, I had a place my body always knew was home.

400 yards. I feel the water hugging me from all angles. My breath begins to slow, evening out.

The memories flow.

Once, one of the older swim team girls told everyone I wasn't really a girl. "She's actually a boy. Can't you see her— *his*," she spat, abruptly changing pronouns, "*his* penis under *his* swimsuit?!" I had yet to discover I was a transgender boy. I was nine, maybe ten, and I didn't have the words to describe myself. "Tomboy" being the closest approximation I had, I walked the world as girl, daughter, sister. I froze as my teammate continued to harass me.

"You're disgusting," the older girl jeered. Her face hardened with anger. Something was dark and twisted about her attack. The boy with her laughed nervously as if to soften the moment.

500 yards. My gender was always a focus of my peers. I was never girl enough to be a girl, and I was never a *real* boy. I was thrown out of bathrooms, taunted by classmates and teachers alike. I eventually concluded that fitting in was not realistic. *I'll just be weird*, I told myself. *That's okay.*

School and other public arenas weren't safe. Underwater, however, I could hide. Underwater, my gender didn't matter. Underwater—for those hours at practice—I didn't even have a body. I was just swimming. And I reveled in that peace.

600 yards. I flip onto my back and kick for a few laps, holding my arms in a streamline above my head. I've always been a strong kicker—maybe due to nature, maybe due to the many injuries I've survived over the years.

In a biking accident before my junior year of high school, I broke my back. The doctors trapped me in a neck-to-hip immobilizing brace and forbade any physical activity. The time away from swim practice was excruciating. My mental health crumbled. Months later, when I dove in for my first practice back, nothing mattered but the feeling of the water rushing past my skin.

But out of the pool, misery loomed. I no longer presented myself as a tomboy; instead, I attempted to be the girl everyone expected me to be—long hair, clothing from the girls' department, makeup, heels. *Maybe this will help me feel better? Maybe I'll finally belong?* I thought. I was wrong.

700 yards. I'm staring at the vaulted ceiling as I continue to kick in a streamline on my back. I hear the buzzer go off for another race, and I lift my head to look at the board. I'll need to finish my warm down soon so I can cheer for the relays.

My final high school race —a regional championship that I'd confidently won—was, unexpectedly, my last in the women's category. Instead of starting college that fall, I entered residential treatment for eating disorders. I couldn't stay that girl I thought I was supposed to be. I teetered on the edge of implosion.

800 yards. Months into treatment, when I was finally permitted to swim again, I'd jumped into a pool murky with too much chlorine. I felt clumsy and out of shape, but the water held me all the same. After, I stood in front of the mirror, tears of anguish streaming down my cheeks. My body had changed quite a bit without constant swimming—its shape uncomfortable and foreign.

And yet, I can still swim. Gratitude flowed forth. *Thank you, body, for all that you do for me.*

900 yards. I push off the wall in a tight streamline, my kicks stronger now that I've flushed out most of the lactic acid. I feel loose and confident. I close my eyes as I break the surface and take a few strokes. I want to remember this feeling—every inch of it.

Before my first race in the men's category, I had stood trying to replicate my pre-meet ritual. As the national anthem played, I searched for my swimsuit strap over my left shoulder, where I always placed my hand.

And then I remembered, in my Speedo, that everything was different.

I no longer had to hide in a women's swimsuit. Now I was me, and only me.

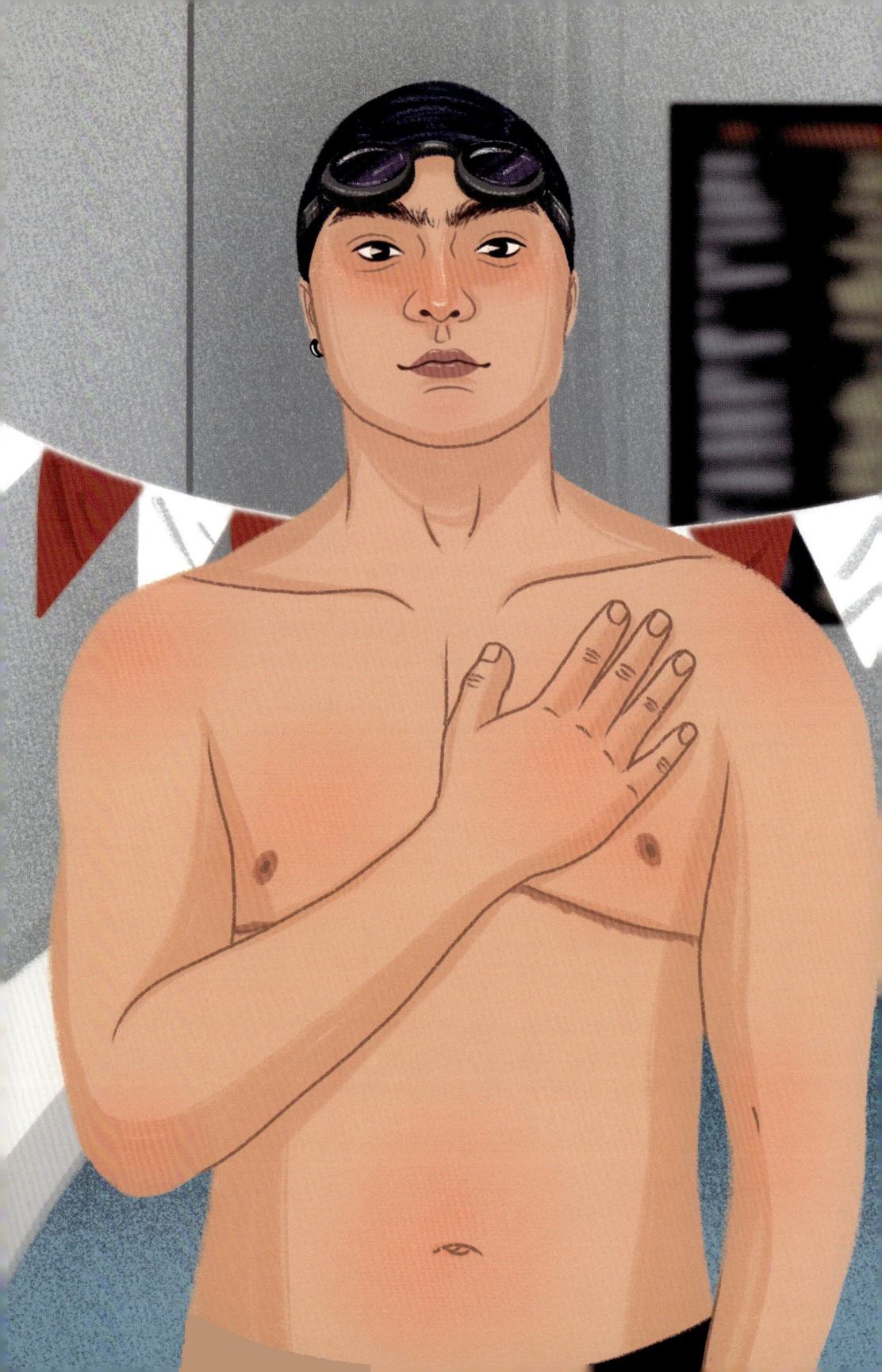

1,000 yards. I switch back to freestyle. I feel light and smooth in the water and my pace quickens.

When I swam my first championship meet on the men's team, I touched the wall and read the board: SCHUYLER BAI-LAR, 59.46. This had been a personal best time by over two seconds, and I was ecstatic. Most of my teammates had gathered next to my lane at the edge of the pool to cheer me on. Upon finishing, their joyful screams were the only thing I could hear.

I had hopped out of the pool, the water beading off my brand-new tech suit. Steven, Hyun-il, and Don were already clapping me on the back as I stood. My walk to the warm down pool was filled with high fives, fist bumps, and more excitement from the guys.

"That's insane, Schuyler, nice job," Steven said as he walked with me. "Wow, what a feeling—the first time under a minute!" For years, I'd dreamed of swimming my 100-yard breaststroke that fast.

"You're dropping time like in age groups!" George said, referring to when we were younger, racing in competitions grouped by age, when improving our personal records was much more common.

"Dude, congratulations, that's huge," Hyun-il said, grinning. He was the best breaststroker on the team. I beamed.

I'd placed last—sixteen out of sixteen—but my teammates knew what my performance meant to me. I was so proud. The glory I felt after that race surpassed any I'd experienced winning in the women's category.

1,100 yards. That race was three years ago. Four years now that I've been on the men's team. A place so many thought I'd never belong—a place in which many thought I'd fail. "From beautiful, competitive woman to mediocre, ugly man," one commenter wrote on a national profile about me my freshman year.

Though I've been lucky to receive support from my team, coaches, parents, and administrators, hatred has still encroached from all angles.

1,200 yards. What has stung most and longest came from the team. After the first year, students get to pick their roommates. We create "blocking groups" that can "link" to other blocking groups and get housed in the same neighborhood of dorms. Since most of my older teammates lived together, I'd assumed that I, too, would block with my swim team class sophomore year.

On the day, the freshmen called a meeting to discuss living arrangements. I was somehow the last to arrive, despite being earlier than the scheduled time.

1,400 yards. "There's no space left for you," one of the guys announced. I looked around the room. No one met my eyes.

Later, I'd learn that one specific guy spearheaded my eviction from the group. He didn't believe I deserved a spot on the team. He found my presence annoying. He feared that my being trans would disrupt the group's dynamic, even scare off potential girlfriends.

He excluded me because I am transgender. He convinced the others to do the same.

I haven't cried such tears of isolation since that night.

OUTCAST, WEIRDO, ALONE, I wrote in my journal.

1,600 yards. The following year, I recorded another best time in my 100-yard breaststroke. Immediately after, some of my teammates crowded around to inform me I'd beaten my team bully. Their grins were bursting with pride. How seen and supported I felt.

1,800 yards. And now today, my final race.

I was so happy to swim next to my best friend, Kevin. We met my second year when he joined the team as a freshman. We bonded quickly after sharing a pull-out couch for a week on our training trip his first semester. Kevin's camaraderie was crucial to my staying on the men's team and getting through college.

Behind the blocks, he gave me a fist bump, smiling with assurance. He knew how nervous I was and what this last race meant to me.

"You got this," he said with a nod.

"We got this," I answered, my chest buzzing with anticipation. As the heat before ours touched the wall, I tugged on the front of my silicone cap to readjust it. I was wearing a Harvard Swimming dome cap—one designed especially for racing, with the Harvard varsity insignia over my ear.

The official's long whistle silenced the natatorium.

This is it.

A short whistle signaled us to step up onto the blocks. As I did, my whole team began to chant my name. "Schuy-ler, Schuy-ler, SCHUY-LER…" growing in volume until they drowned out all other sounds.

This was it. *This* was where I belonged. In this pool, with these swimmers, next to Kevin. It didn't matter who else thought I was supposed to be there. *I* knew. For that moment, *this* was the only place I was ever supposed to be. Right there. Right then.

I dove in.

Schuyler Bailar dives into Harvard's Blodgett Pool in Boston, Massachusetts, on November 6, 2023.

2,000 yards. I'm almost finished with my warm down. One final stroke. I focus on the catch—grabbing the water to pull myself forward. I touch the wall with both hands, outstretched in a streamline. I pull off my cap and dunk my head, feeling the cool water stream through my hair.

I hop out of the pool.

I walk to our team area, my whole life ahead of me.

Lia Thomas

FIGHTING IN THE POOL, AND OUT OF IT

"It's not a women's sport if it doesn't include ALL women." —The American Civil Liberties Union

You can't talk about trans women's rights in athletics without talking about Lia Thomas. A transgender swimmer who competed on the University of Pennsylvania's women's team, Lia is often considered the face of the debate on transgender women in sports. A swimmer since she was five years old, Lia first competed on the University of Pennsylvania's men's team in 2017 when she arrived there as a freshman.

Though she started hormone therapy in 2019 and came out as trans that fall, Lia was still confined to the men's team. She has spoken about how awkward and uncomfortable it was, and how her competitive speed suffered because of the way her muscles weakened during the hormone therapy. At that time, the NCAA required that transgender athletes complete one year of hormone replacement therapy to be cleared to compete. Lia submitted her medical documentation accordingly and was approved to swim for the women's team the following season.

This did not unfold without controversy. Though Lia's competitive times have all dropped in speed since she transitioned, some people believe she has an unfair advantage in the sport.

That being said, Lia also received tremendous support against this backlash. In 2022, three hundred current and former NCAA swimmers signed a letter stating that they stood with Lia and all trans and nonbinary athletes. "With this letter, we express our support for Lia Thomas, and all transgender college athletes, who deserve to be able to participate in safe and welcoming athletic environments," it read.

Despite the controversy, Lia has no regrets.

"I just want to show trans kids and younger trans athletes that they're not alone. They don't have to choose between who they are and the sport they love." —LIA THOMAS, in *Sports Illustrated*

Lia graduated in 2022 and plans to attend law school and pursue a career as a civil rights attorney. She has taken legal action against World Aquatics for its rule in 2022 that prohibits anyone who has undergone "any part of male puberty" from the female category. Lia's stance is that this rule is discriminatory, and she hopes to make a change for future transgender swimmers.

Courtesy of Iszac Henig

Iszac Henig (left), Lia Thomas (center), and Schuyler Bailar (right), pictured here in 2023, are former collegiate swimmers who competed in the Ivy League after receiving hormone replacement therapy as part of gender affirmation care.

RUNNING MY HEART OUT
BY CECÉ TELFER

Now

I should be at indoor Nationals, but the rules aren't exactly *for* me right now. So even if I did go, or I did run the time… they just won't take me.

I don't know what to do.

Then

I run because it's freeing.

I run not only because it's where I can cause that change I want to see in the world, but also because it makes me feel human. Like I have a purpose. It makes me feel like this is something that I can do.

This is my purpose in life. Everyone has their career, their jobs, their reason, and this is mine. I couldn't go after my calling when I was younger—little CeCé didn't know she could do it—so I'm doing it for her.

I was bullied at a young age by everybody. People would ask my family, "Is that a girl or a boy?" They would call me names because I was very feminine. I thought I was going to become my mom and sister. I thought I was going to bloom into them one day.

As a kid, I was very innocent, very extroverted. I just wanted love. I wasn't aggressive. I don't do violence. I observed. I mimicked—I'm a really good mimicker.

Mimicking is how I became an athlete, how I picked up sports so easily. I mimic good things that change the world.

I came out as trans in high school, and I struggled most around what to do with athletics.

I didn't want to come out publicly in athletics because I didn't know what would happen. I didn't want to sacrifice my one safe haven and saving grace, so I had a lot of thinking to do.

When I came out in college, my teammates overall were supportive. Of course, not everyone is going to love you. Not everyone is going to approve. A lot of the negative things that were said weren't said to my face.

But my coaches were 100 percent supportive—300 percent supportive, even. When I went to them and told them, their response was, "*Finally.*"

It was kind of beautiful in that sense. "Finally. We've been waiting. We saw you. We saw CeCé," they said.

What did it feel like to be seen?

Unfamiliar.

Shocking.

Warm.

I just was not expecting it. I went into the room with my authentic self and my friend, ready to tell my coach off. Prepared to say, "This is who I am, you're not going to change me no matter what you do." I was ready to fight.

So to then have that adrenaline shut down with love, acceptance, and embrace...I was confused! I was like, *Oh my God, wait, I could have been me this whole time? I wish someone had said something!* It was emotional. Very emotional. A lot of tears and happiness.

That moment confirmed that I could be *me*, 100 percent. When I had first gotten to Franklin Pierce University, day one of orientation, I was starting over, taking the initiative to be full CeCé. But even so, I still hadn't been fully myself in the gym, on the court, in the locker rooms. I hadn't been fully me. It was *that* moment, that validation from my coaches, where I finally felt, *I don't have to pretend anymore.* And, oh my gosh, it changed *everything.*

For me to have this realization that *I don't care, and I'm ready to live?*

It was...beautiful.

Now

People think my journey is the same as every other woman who happens to be transgender, which is so far from the truth. I have muscles, and I'm tall, and I'm Black. I have strong masculine features, so people make a certain association.

I am tall and I look strong, but the rules and the protocols I have to follow make me feel so far from it. I'm the true definition of *looks are so deceiving*.

The constrictions applied in order for me to be a professional athlete are depleting my body. Diminishing my strength. My talent. My God-given reason. They're taking away from me.

The "even playing field" narrative that is being created to "deal with" transgender athletes? *We* suffer the medical consequences. It's killing me softly, and people think that it's okay because I signed off on it, because I "chose" this.

That's the frustrating part—the idea that *you signed up for this, so whatever happens, happens.*

There isn't any research yet into the long-term effects of what hormone suppression does to a body like mine, but nobody cares, because it's a rule—something that is put into place to govern bodies like my own.

So why even compete? Why am I doing it?

I'm not only doing this for me and my dreams, but for the generations to come. The kids who are looking up to someone like me, the little girls who happen to be trans, and for all the little CeCés out there who see this as a livelihood, something lifesaving. I compete so they know they can do this as well. They can reach the highest level of sport.

You have to see a physical manifestation of your dreams in order to achieve them. I don't have that, I didn't have that. But I can be that for the little CeCés looking up.

Whenever I'm crying and want to quit—because every single day I'm my own doctor, I'm my own coach, my own physical therapist, my own nutritionist, and I'm the athlete; I have to be so disciplined in *everything*, and it does take a toll on me, and I don't have supporters around to remind me to keep going—*that's* why I keep going.

If it were easy, everyone would do it. I just gotta keep going until I get there, and 2024 is my year. I'm going to Paris. I'm making the Olympic team. If I don't make Team USA, I'm competing under the Olympic flag.

I'm running my heart out, I'm leaving everything on the track, and I have to, need to, *must* go to Paris this summer.

A lot of people don't understand that to be an elite athlete, a champion, an Olympian, the greatest of all time—a GOAT— you need somebody seeing, breathing, supporting, believing, and living that dream with you.

That manifestation, that's all you, yes, but you need that other person. I don't have family members, friends, aunties, or uncles to do that. There are supporters who donate, they do their part. But I don't have that blood, that die-hard, that "I'm

CeCé Telfer running, midstride.

traveling with you, I'm making sure you're good at meets." I don't have that dreamer with me.

It's all on me, and that makes it so much harder.

Especially in moments when I'm watching my counterparts compete at Nationals, and I'm not there. But I deserve to be there. I have the times, I'm up there. Every single track meet I've been to this year, I'm the girl to beat. I've been bringing the competition, yet I still don't have the tools to get to where I need to be.

Then, on top of everything, we need to worry about our bodies and what we look like and what that's presenting—God forbid everything isn't right and tight and looking like my cisgender counterparts. Even if it is, people rooting against me are going to think that it's not. They're looking for everything. First: crotch. They're looking for the bulge.

Which is really sad! It's like, our clothes are getting skimpier and skimpier! They expect us to run in underwear and a crop top, and if I did (which I would actually love because it's freeing), society would kill me.

Let's be honest. Every time I go to track meets, every time I leave my house, I don't have the privacy to get my stuff done and stand on business, because everyone is looking at me. Had I had the privilege of that private lifestyle, I'd probably have made the team. Had I had someone to advocate for me, I would have made the team. The Olympics would have been cake.

But I don't have that.

How are you finding someone a threat simply for being their real selves? They aren't hiding who they are, they aren't harming anyone, and you're compelled to hurt them?

No matter how hard we try, as trans athletes, sometimes nothing is ever enough.

And at the end of the day, no one cares about women's sports. Because if they did, they'd make sure they had good research before imposing treatments on our bodies. They'd make sure we had equal pay. They'd make sure we had the things that we've been crying about since the dawn of time, and they would see us.

But the world doesn't see us. What needs to change?

The focus of elite sports has drifted from creating history to making money. Coaches don't care about civil rights, change, making a difference, equality, inclusion, and diversity. They want the best athlete to get them that Nike contract, to get them that job.

And I have to put myself in their shoes, because it's not that I'm not good enough. My talents are being diminished every day, and I'm still up there with my times. So what am I doing wrong? What is the catch? It's money. It's capitalism.

What needs change is the way coaches get paid, but also their mindset. They need sensitivity training, and they need to be able to

create safe spaces for athletes like me. They have to know how to handle these situations, regardless of sexual orientation, gender identity, race, and class. They must be equipped to tackle change, and difference, and anything else they might not be used to.

They need to educate themselves.

Because it's unfair for athletes' talent and humanity to be neglected just because of their sexual orientation or how they identify.

The Future

What about you? What can you do?

You can be aware of current events and what's going on in the world, especially in athletics. You can be very mindful, especially if you're a team captain, of everything that is going on, so that when a ban comes out from World Athletics, you can say, "We aren't going to stand for this." You can learn to educate people, starting with your team, with your coaches, and let goodness branch out from there.

Create a safe space from the get-go. From day one, nip exclusion in the bud.

Stand up and say, "We don't tolerate discrimination of any kind. I don't want to be part of a team that tolerates hate."

That's somewhere to start.

EDITOR'S NOTE

In 2023, on March 31—widely known as Transgender Day of Visibility—World Athletics put a rule into effect that bans athletes who have gone through "male puberty" from participating in female world-ranking competitions. "Decisions are always difficult when they involve conflicting needs and rights between different groups, but we continue to take the view that we must maintain fairness for female athletes above all other considerations," World Athletics president Sebastian Coe had said in a statement.

In a response, Hudson Taylor, founder and executive director of the advocacy group Athlete Ally, said, "We are beyond devastated to see World Athletics succumbing to political pressure instead of core principles of inclusion, fairness and non-discrimination for transgender athletes and athletes with intersex variations."

This rule directly impacts athletes like CeCé Telfer, banning her from competing in her sport.

Megan Rapinoe

PROFESSIONAL ACTIVIST, LEGENDARY SOCCER PLAYER, AND PROUD QUEER WOMAN

It's hard to distill the magic of Megan Rapinoe into a single category.

You could, of course, start on the soccer field. Megan, who began playing when she was a kid, would go on to win two Women's World Cups, in 2015 and 2019, a gold medal at the 2012 London Olympics, and a bronze medal at the 2020 Tokyo Olympics. In 2019, she was also named Women's Player of the Year by the Fédération Internationale de Football Association (FIFA). These accolades, among others—including an impressive National Women's Soccer League career—make her one of soccer's most accomplished and recognizable players.

You could also talk about her activism, which is what Megan ultimately wants to be remembered for. In an article for the *Chicago Sun-Times*, Megan said, "By a mile, what we've done off the field [is what I'll be most proud of]. That has made a lasting impact." These moments of activism did not come without controversy and backlash—people telling Megan to just play soccer instead of speaking out—but that never held Megan back from doing what she felt was right.

In 2016, she became the first white athlete to kneel during the national anthem, a movement started by professional football player Colin Kaepernick to protest racism and police brutality against African Americans. In 2019, Megan joined several of her teammates in a lawsuit against the U.S. Soccer

Federation, fighting for equal pay to that of the US men's soccer team—a lawsuit that ended with the federation promising equal pay for the men's and women's teams at future events.

"You have a responsibility to use whatever talent you have, or whatever way you can, to make the world a better place." —MEGAN RAPINOE

Megan's name is synonymous with soccer excellence and social justice. But it's impossible to appraise her total impact without talking about how essential she has been to the LGBTQ+ community, too. "For a long time, I was the only player that was out," Megan said to *Time* magazine. She came out publicly in 2012, right before the London Olympics, where she and her team would win gold.

Ever since, Megan has taken her platform seriously and constantly pushed for LGBTQ+ equal rights. "I still, to this day, have people coming up to me or writing me or whatever it may be, you know, thanking me or saying, you know, I'm the reason they felt okay with themselves or I'm the reason their family was okay," said Megan. "They see themselves in me."

Megan is not just a soccer player, or just a queer woman, or just an activist. She is all of these things, and she has worked hard throughout her entire career to be outspoken and the best version of herself in all of these identities. She has paved the way for women's athletics, for queer people, for activism in service of equality for all.

EPILOGUE

Sometimes the sports we love might not love us back. At the time of our writing this, over 30 percent of the LGBTQ+ population live in states that have laws preventing transgender students from participating in sports teams consistent with their gender identity. It is our greatest hope that the rules and laws that we've discussed throughout these pages become outdated—that they be declared discriminatory, and wrong. That someday the painful content in this book becomes history, rather than persisting as deep-seated issues facing LGBTQ+ athletes.

Because the truth of the matter is that LGBTQ+ athletes have always competed in sports. So much so that this book could not have included everyone. Not even close. For example, we didn't include the following:

NHL player **Luke Prokop,**
tennis professional **Renee Richards,**
NFL athlete **Michael Sam,**
WNBA star **Sue Bird,**
NBA athlete **Jason Paul Collins**,
soccer player **Robbie Rogers,**
professional boxer **Patricio Manuel,**
Olympic weight lifter **Laurel Hubbard**,
MMA fighter **Fallon Fox,**
MLB player **Glenn Burke**.

The list goes on and on and on. We promise.

If you are a queer athlete: You are not alone. If you are part of the LGBTQ+ community and you want to play a sport but don't know where to start, we hope that this book gave you an idea. If you are playing a sport and are struggling with balancing your love of that sport with your identity, know that there are other athletes just like you who have struggled, too, but who have also found joy, and who are working to carve out those safe spaces in sports for all of us.

What it comes down to is this: We, as athletes, are everywhere. We deserve to be everywhere. And we can excel everywhere, too.

ABOUT THE CONTRIBUTORS

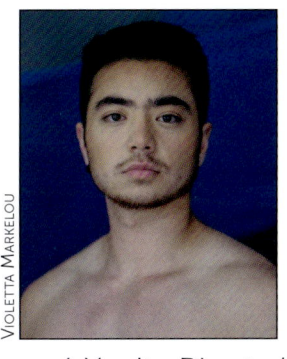

VIOLETTA MARKELOU

SCHUYLER BAILAR (he/him) is an educator, author, and advocate. He is also the first openly transgender athlete to compete in any sport on an NCAA Division I men's team. Schuyler's exemplary work has earned him numerous honors including NYC Pride Grand Marshal, inclusion in the Out100 list, LGBTQ Nation's Instagram Advocate of the Year, and the Harvard Varsity Director's Award. In addition to being a top LGBTQ+ educator and advocate, Schuyler is the creator of the groundbreaking LaneChanger.com gender literacy online learning series. He holds a degree in cognitive neuroscience and evolutionary psychology from Harvard and works in four research labs focusing in clinical psychology and public health.

JENNIFER BUHL

ERIK J. BROWN is the *USA Today bestselling* author of *All That's Left in the World*, *The Only Light Left Burning*, and *Lose You to Find Me*, and the cohost of the young adult book podcast *YA-Okay*. His genre-blending books have received starred reviews from *Kirkus Reviews*, *Booklist*, and *School Library Journal*. He's also six foot five, but even if he didn't have terrible hand-eye coordination and reflexes, he probably still wouldn't be a professional athlete because he's very accident-prone. He lives in Philadelphia with his family.

em dickson (e/em/eir/she) is a school librarian, authenticity reader, competitive sailor, and, according to eir friends, sea shanty royale extraordinaire. E holds a dual MA/MFA in children's literature and writing for children and young adults from Simmons University and has written for preschool IP under the name Em Lune. Like Peter Pan, e has a strong emotional attachment to eir shadow, a fluffy black Muppet of a dog called Luna, and e definitely believes in ghosts, witches, and especially selkies. When not reading or writing, e can be found daydreaming, accidentally harmonizing to random sounds, collecting trinkets in eir pockets like a dragon, or promoting the color teal. E feels most at home by the sea, which is convenient, since e spends most of eir time in coastal Massachusetts. E invites you to em @mlereads.

JACK FERNANDES is a transmasc enby from New England who has been playing hockey since he was seven years old. He has played all positions in hockey and comes from a family of goalies-by-choice! He played on coed teams, girls' teams, and boys' teams from age seven to sixteen and then started it all over again at nineteen in the New York City Gay Hockey Association. He has worked in professional women's ice hockey with the Connecticut Whale and currently works at a hockey rink.

ISAAC FITZSIMONS (fits-EYE-mons) writes so that every reader can see themselves reflected in literature. His debut novel, *The Passing Playbook*, received numerous accolades including being named a Junior Library Guild Gold Standard Selection, a Summer/Fall 2021 Indies Introduce title, a *Kirkus* Best Young Adult Book of 2021, and a 2022 Lambda

Literary Award finalist. Isaac has previously dabbled in performing sketch comedy and learning how to play three songs on the banjo. His dream vacation would be to travel around Europe via sleeper train and see every top-tier soccer team play a home game. He currently lives outside Washington, DC.

COURTESY OF IZ FUERTER

IZ FUERTER (they/them) is a dedicated member of both the New York City Gay Hockey Association and Trans Wave, bringing their passion for ice hockey and inclusivity together. When not on the ice, they enjoy immersing themselves in books and connecting with nature.

DYLAN FURLANO

KATHERINE LOCKE lives and writes in Philadelphia, Pennsylvania, with their feisty felines. They are the award-winning author of many books for kids and teens, including *Gender Rebels* and *What Are Your Words?*; they are also a coeditor and contributor for *This Is Our Rainbow: 16 Stories of Her, Him, Them, Us*. They can be found online @bibliogato on X and Instagram and at katherinelockebooks.com.

COURTESY OF KARINA MANTA

KARINA MANTA is a writer and professional figure skater. She is the author of the young adult memoir *On Top of Glass*. Despite being raised in the desert of Chandler, Arizona, she fell in love with ice dancing and spent several years competing as a member of Team USA. Since leaving the competitive skating world, she has had numerous professional skating jobs, such as touring with Cirque du Soleil and performing on British reality television. She resides in Brooklyn, New York, and invites you to visit her online at karinamanta.com.

NICOLE MELLEBY, a New Jersey native, is the author of highly praised middle-grade books, including the Lambda Literary Award finalist *Hurricane Season*, ALA Notable book *How to Become a Planet*, *Camp QUILTBAG* (cowritten with A. J. Sass), and the House on Sunrise Lagoon series. She is also the author of the picture book *Sunny and Oswaldo*. Nicole lives with her wife and their cats, whose need for attention oddly aligns with Nicole's writing schedule. She invites you to visit her online at nicolemelleby.com.

QUINCE MOUNTAIN is an adventure athlete and wilderness guide who enjoys survival challenges and spending time with his family and team of sled dogs. He was the first openly trans competitor in the Iditarod sled dog race.

MARIEKE NIJKAMP (she/they) is the author of the Splinter & Ash series, *Ink Girls* with Sylvia Bi, and many other books for all ages, including *New York Times* bestsellers, a critically acclaimed anthology, graphic novels, and comics. She studied philosophy and medieval history, and when she isn't writing, she loves to watch sports, garden, roll dice, and daydream. Marieke lives and writes in Small Town, the Netherlands. She invites you to visit her online at mariekenijkamp.com/musings/.

AARON JAY

ADAM RIPPON is an Olympic athlete and medal-winning figure skater. He won the 2010 Four Continents Championships and the 2016 U.S. Figure Skating Championships and was selected to represent the United States at the 2018 Winter Olympics in Pyeongchang, South Korea. He came out as gay in October 2015 and, at the 2018 Winter Olympics, won a bronze medal as part of the figure skating team event, thus becoming the first openly gay US male athlete to win a medal in a Winter Olympics. Later that year, he was named to the *Time* 100 Most Influential People list, *Forbes* 30 Under 30, *Adweek's* Creative 100, and *Out* magazine's Power 50. He won season twenty-six of *Dancing with the Stars* before going on to be a judge on the premiere season of *Dancing with the Stars: Juniors*. He is the author of *Beautiful on the Outside: A Memoir.*

DEVEN SASS-CAO

A. J. SASS (he/they) is the author of the ALA Rainbow Book List Top 10 titles *Ellen Outside the Lines,* which was also a Sydney Taylor Honor Book; *Ana on the Edge; Just Shy of Ordinary;* as well as *Camp QUILTBAG* (cowritten with Nicole Melleby). A longtime figure skater, he has passed his U.S. Figure Skating Senior Moves in the Field and Free Skate tests, has medaled twice at the U.S. Synchronized Skating Championships, and currently dabbles in ice dance. He lives in the San Francisco Bay Area with his husband and two cats who act like dogs. He invites you to visit him online at sassinsf.com.

ALBERT TANG

CECÉ TELFER is a Jamaican American elite athlete who, in June 2019, became the first openly transgender woman to win an NCAA national title. Telfer became an NCAA national champion in the 400-meter hurdles, which put her on the trajectory of becoming a US Olympic hopeful for the 2020 and 2024 Games. Telfer also competes in the 60-meter, 100-meter, and 200-meter. In June 2021, Telfer qualified for the 2020 U.S. Olympic Team Trials—Track & Field in the 100-meter and 400-meter hurdles. Unfortunately, new rulings from World Athletics have made Telfer ineligible for Olympic Trials. Despite this, Telfer pushes forward, continuing to train, and is fighting to get back onto the world stage. She is the author of the adult memoir *Make It Count: My Fight to Become the First Transgender Olympic Runner.*

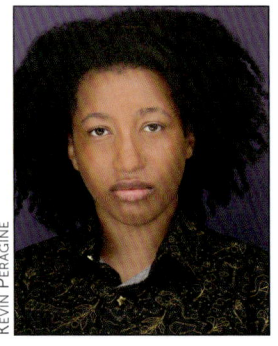

KEVIN PERAGINE

VINCENT TIRADO is a nonbinary Afro Latine Bronx native. Their first novel, *Burn Down, Rise Up,* was a Pura Belpré Award winner, a Bram Stoker Award finalist, and a Lambda Literary Award finalist. They are also the author of *We Don't Swim Here, We Came to Welcome You*, and a short story in the horror anthology *The Black Girl Survives in This One*. When Vincent is not busy being a menace to society, you can find them harassing their cat, Bugsy. They invite you to visit their website, v-e-tirado.com.

ALEX PAYAN

JESS VOSSETEIG (Jess Voss Art) is a queer illustrator and writer born and raised in Colorado. Partnering with brands and organizations like Dr. Martens, Lush, Ulta, the Ms. Foundation for Women, Facebook/Meta, and more, their work focuses on inclusivity, empowerment, and creating conversations surrounding feminism and the queer community. Jess loves illustrating to empower all genders, break stereotypes, and promote body positivity/neutrality. Jess wants their audience to feel seen and heard in their work, be empowered to be themselves, educate others, and push societal norms. Jess invites you to find more of their work and shop at jessvossart.com and @JessVoss_Art.

DAWN ENNIS

KARLEIGH WEBB is an award-winning journalist who has worked as a reporter, anchor, sportscaster, videographer, and network-television producer. An out trans woman, she is also an activist for intersectional justice across her professional and personal lives. She regularly contributes to the LGBTQ+ sports site Outsports.com and also works for Trans Lifeline, North America's only twenty-four-hour crisis line founded and operated by transgender people. A lifelong athlete, Karleigh is an avid marathoner, cyclist, and triathlete who's equally at home on a football or softball field. She plays football through the Women's Football Alliance, alternating positions between running back, linebacker, and defensive end.

HOW TO BE A GOOD TEAMMATE AND ALLY

Don't assume that you have no LGBTQ+ players on your team. Many players aren't out to their friends, teammates, and coaches. Make sure your team remains a safe space whether or not you know if your teammates are part of the LGBTQ+ community.

Do get educated on the experiences and challenges that LGBTQ+ athletes face. The more you know, the more you'll be able to recognize and help your fellow teammates when needed.

Do develop an inclusive team code of conduct so you can create a safe space that recognizes every player is a valuable member of your team.

Do use inclusive language when talking to and around your teammates. We don't always realize that some of the common sayings and phrases used in sports come from sexist, homophobic, transphobic, racist, or ableist ideas. Use phrases like, "Welcome, everyone" instead of "Welcome, boys and/or girls" so you don't misgender or exclude nonbinary teammates. Avoid negative phrases like "Man up," and instead use empowering language such as "You've got this!"

Do support your transgender and nonbinary teammates by asking all teammates for their pronouns before making assumptions. Respect your teammates by using the pronouns and names they ask you to use.

Don't look the other way when a teammate is being harassed or bullied. Let the bully know that they are being homophobic, transphobic, disrespectful, or unsupportive, and find a coach or administrator to talk to.

Do hold your teammates—and yourself—accountable and always apologize and try to be better when you make mistakes.

WHAT MAKES YOU FEEL STRONG?

> **STRONG (ADJECTIVE)**
> 1. having great physical power and ability: having a lot of strength
> 2. not easy to break or damage
>
> —*Merriam-Webster.com Dictionary*

WHAT MAKES YOU FEEL STRONG?

Do you have to win to feel strong?

Can a team that always loses still feel strong?

Do you need to be the biggest or fastest on your team to be strong?

Can you be the smallest or slowest on your team and still be strong?

Do you need to be able to lift heavy things to be strong?

Is being strong always a physical experience?

Does being strong mean performing perfectly or never making a mistake?

Are you allowed to feel nervous or anxious while competing and still be strong?

Can you be afraid and still be strong?

If you aren't strong, then are you weak?

If you feel weak, can you still be strong?

ATTENTION ALL ATHLETES

**Want to form your own Queer Athletics Alliance
or Gender and Sexuality Alliance in your school?
Here are ten steps to getting started.**

1. **Follow the Rules**

   Your school should have guidelines on how to start
   a new club or extracurricular. Consult your school's
   student handbook or its website to learn what these
   rules and guidelines are.

2. **Find an Advisor**

   Ask a teacher, coach, or other faculty member at
   your school who you think would be supportive and
   who has proven themselves to be an ally to LGBTQ+
   students.

3. **Recruit Other Students**

   Invite your friends, classmates, teammates, and other
   athletes in your school who would be interested in
   joining and building this LGBTQ+ safe space.

4. **Inform Your Administration**

   Let the administration at your school know what you
   are doing right away. It's always good to have their

help on your side. If an administrator opposes your Queer Athletics Alliance or Gender and Sexuality Alliance (GSA), know your rights. If you attend a public school in the United States that allows other clubs, the administration must allow you to start a GSA, too. You can provide them additional information at glsen.org.

5. Pick a Meeting Place

Do you prefer somewhere accessible in your school that offers privacy? Or do you want a space out in the open, to attract more members? Consider what makes the most sense for you and your fellow club members.

6. Advertise

Here's where you bring out the rainbows! Get creative and think about the best forms of community outreach, whether it's in your school bulletin, announcements, flyers, or word of mouth.

7. Plan Your Meeting

Identify what you want to accomplish during your meetings. There are tons of things to consider: You can have discussions, invite speakers, hold workshops, play games. This is *your* club; think about why you're starting it and what you want from your new safe space.

8. Hold Your First Meeting

Perhaps you might launch your first meeting with a conversation about why you all think this group is important or needed. Alternatively, use your first meeting to brainstorm with your members on ways to use your club moving forward.

9. Establish a Mission Statement

Coming up with ground rules helps to ensure that group discussions and activities are safe, confidential, and respectful.

10. Plan for the Future

Set goals for what you want to work toward over the course of the school year.

Starting a student organization can be difficult, between researching your school's guidelines for starting a new club, finding a faculty or coach advisor, understanding your rights as an LGBTQ+ student and student athlete, writing a mission statement, and, of course, recruiting members and hosting your first meeting. The Gay, Lesbian & Straight Education Network (GLSEN) website has all this information and more. Check it out and build your own team alliance today: glsen.org/support-student-gsas.

SELECTED SOURCES

INTRODUCTION

The Trevor Project. "LGBTQ Youth Sports Participation."
September 15, 2021.
https://www.thetrevorproject.org/research-briefs/lgbtq-youth
-sports-participation-2/.

A NOTE ON PRONOUNS

UT News. "Using Chosen Names Reduces Odds of Depression and
Suicide in Transgender Youths." Health & Wellness. March 18,
2018. https://news.utexas.edu/2018/03/30/name-use-matters-for
-transgender-youths-mental-health/.

WHAT IS TITLE IX? AND WHY DOES IT MATTER?

Alexander, Kerri Lee. "Bernice Sandler (1928–2019)." National
Women's History Museum. Accessed March 2024.
https://www.womenshistory.org/education-resources/biographies/
bernice-sandler.

Palumbo, Laura. "10 Facts Everyone Should Know About Title IX."
National Sexual Violence Resource Center. August 23, 2017.
https://www.nsvrc.org/blogs/10-facts-everyone-should-know-about
-title-ix.

U.S. Department of Education. "FACT SHEET: U.S. Department
of Education's Proposed Change to Its Title IX Regulations on
Students' Eligibility for Athletic Teams." April 6, 2023.
https://www.ed.gov/news/press-releases/fact-sheet-us-department
-educations-proposed-change-its-title-ix-regulations-students
-eligibility-athletic-teams.

GET TO KNOW AUGUSTUS "GUS" KENWORTHY

GB Snowsport. "Gus Kenworthy on Being the First Olympic Skier to Come Out." Accessed March 2024. https://gbsnowsport.com/gus -kenworthy-on-being-the-first-olympic-skier-to-come-out/.

Roenigk, Alyssa. "Olympic Freeskier Gus Kenworthy's Next Bold Move—Coming Out." ESPN. October 22, 2015. https://www.espn .com/olympics/story/_/id/13942305/olympic-freeskier-x-games-star -gus-kenworthy-first-openly-gay-action-sports-athlete.

"Skier: My Coming Out Story Is My Olympic Legacy." Interview by Coy Wire. CNN. Accessed March 2024. Video, 3:25. https://www.cnn.com/videos/sports/2022/02/16/gus-kenworthy -winter-olympics-wire-intvu-intl-ovn-vpx.cnn.

HOCKEY IS FOR EVERYONE: A Conversation with Jack Fernandes and Iz Fuerter of the New York City Gay Hockey Association

Branch, Jon. "In Rarity, a Player Speaks Out for Gay Rights." *New York Times*. May 7, 2011. https://www.nytimes .com/2011/05/08/sports/hockey/08avery.html.

Chappell, Bill. "NHL Lifts Ban on Rainbow-Colored Pride Tape, After a Player Defied It." National Public Radio. October 25, 2023. https://www.npr.org/2023/10/25/1208403697/nhl-pride-tape-ban -lifted-travis-dermottwww.nycgha.org.

GET TO KNOW COURTNEY VANDERSLOOT AND ALLIE QUIGLEY

Niesen, Joan. "Meet the Vanderquigs: How the Chicago Sky Stars Make Their Unique Relationship Work." *Sports Illustrated*. July, 25, 2019. https://www.si.com/wnba/2019/07/25/chicago-sky -vandersloot-quigley-marriage-helps-basketball-life.

Quigley, Allie. "The 7 Best Shooters in the WNBA Playoffs. Period." The Players' Tribune. August 21, 2018. https://www.theplayerstribune .com/articles/wnba-allie-quigley-7-best-shooters-period.

Smith, Michelle. "Allie Quigley's Underdog Story." ESPN. September 5, 2014. https://www.espn.com/wnba/story/_/id/11471318/from -waiver-wire-winning-awards-allie-quigley-underdog-story.

Trimmer, Dave. "Gonzaga and Courtney Vandersloot: Perfect Match." *The Spokesman-Review.* March 12, 2011. https://www.spokesman .com/stories/2011/mar/12/gonzaga-and-courtney-vandersloot -perfect-match/.

GET TO KNOW CARL NASSIB

Belson, Ken. "Raiders' Carl Nassib Announces He's Gay, an N.F.L. First." *New York Times.* Updated September 14, 2021. https://www.nytimes.com/2021/06/21/sports/football/carl-nassib -gay-nfl.html.

OSullivan, Brendan. "What Happened to Carl Nassib? The Story of NFL's First Active Gay Player and Where He Is Today." *The Sporting News.* April 26, 2024. https://www.sportingnews .com/us/nfl/news/carl-nassib-story-nfl-first-active-gay -player/042ab00f14a8ddd2bcef6902#:~:text=Carl%20Nassib%20 shocked%20the%20world,while%20on%20an%20active%20 roster.

Patra, Kevin. "Carl Nassib, First Active NFL Player to Come Out as Gay, Announces Retirement from Football." NFL. September 6, 2023. https://www.nfl.com/news/carl-nassib-retires-first-active -nfl-player-to-come-out-as-gay.

GET TO KNOW BILLIE JEAN KING

Women's Sports Foundation. "Billie Jean King, Megan Rapinoe, and Candace Parker Join Nearly 200 Athletes Supporting Trans Youth Participation in Sports." December 21, 2020. https://www .womenssportsfoundation.org/press_release/billie-jean-king-megan -rapinoe-and-candace-parker-join-nearly-200-athletes-supporting -trans-youth-participation-in-sports/.

GET TO KNOW ELLIA GREEN

Holmes, Jon. "Olympic Gold Medalist Ellia Green Says Speaking About Being Trans Gives Him Joy." Outsports. January 5, 2024 https://www.outsports.com/2024/1/5/24026037/ellia-green -olympics-transgender-coming-out-lgbtq-podcast/.

Passa, Dennis. "'I'd Like to Help Someone by Telling My Story':
Green Finds Liberation in Transition." Sydney Morning Herald.
August 17, 2022. https://www.smh.com.au/sport/
rugby-union/i-d-like-to-help-someone-by-telling-my-story-green
-finds-liberation-in-transition-20220817-p5bagm.html.

GET TO KNOW LIA THOMAS

Athlete Alley. "300+ NCAA , Team USA & Olympic Swimmers: We
Support Lia and All Trans & Nonbinary Athletes." February 10,
2022. https://www.athleteally.org/300-swimmers-support-lia/.

Close, David, and Emma Tucker. "Transgender Swimmer Lia Thomas
Begins Legal Case Against Swimming's World Governing
Body." CNN. Updated January 26, 2024. https://www.cnn
.com/2024/01/26/us/lia-thomas-world-aquatics-transgender
-athletes-swimming/index.html.

Sanchez, Robert. "'I Am Lia': The Trans Swimmer Dividing America
Tells Her Story." *Sports Illustrated.* March 3, 2022. https://www
.si.com/college/2022/03/03/lia-thomas-penn-swimmer-transgender
-woman-daily-cover.

GET TO KNOW MEGAN RAPINOE

Bregman, Scott. "Megan Rapinoe's visibility shines a light for the
LGBTQ+ community." Olympics. June 1, 2023. https://olympics
.com/en/news/megan-rapinoe-lgbtq-community-inspiration.

Costabile, Annie. "Megan Rapinoe Reflects on Career with
USWNT Ahead of Final Match at Soldier Field." *Chicago
Sun-Times.* September 23, 2023. https://chicago.suntimes.com/
soccer/2023/9/23/23886888/megan-rapinoe-reflects-on-career-with
-uswnt-ahead-of-final-match-at-soldier-field.

Mikkelsen, Sebastian, and Will Imbo. "USWNT legend Megan
Rapinoe: All titles, Awards, Stats and Records—Complete List."
Olympics. Updated November 12, 2023. https://olympics.com/en/
news/uswnt-legend-megan-rapinoe-all-titles-awards-stats-records
-complete-list.

ACKNOWLEDGMENTS

We are so grateful for every one of our contributors for their time, energy, vulnerability, and passionate belief in a better world for queer athletes across the world. This collection came together because of all of you. You amaze us. Thank you.

Thank you to Katherine's dad for the spark that turned this idea into this book. Four years later, here it is! We hope you love it.

Thank you to our agents, Jim McCarthy and Lara Perkins, for being champions of both of us and of this book, through the ups and downs. We can't imagine better partners.

Thank you to Jessica Anderson, our fearless editor, who saw the potential in this idea from the beginning and sat us down to say, "What if..." and *Athlete Is Agender* was born. This anthology has taken some extra steering, support, and love, and, Jessica: We knew that we were safe in your hands and that our contributors were safe in your hands. Thank you for everything. It has been an utter joy.

Thank you to Jess Vosseteig for beautifully illustrating this book. The art is *gorgeous*, and we are obsessed with it. You made this book come to life, and we appreciate it.

Thank you to Carla Weise, Jenny Kimura, Marisa Finkelstein, Kerianne Steinberg, Sarah Vostok, Jonathan Lopes, Hannah Klein, Andie Divelbiss, Mara Brashem, and Victoria Stapleton for all your hard work creating this book and getting it into the hands of readers. Books couldn't happen without you, and we are so lucky that you are on *Athlete Is Agender*'s team!

And of course, we're grateful for each other. This is the second anthology we've done together, and you learn new things with each one. *Athlete Is Agender* was truly a labor of love, and we couldn't have done it without supporting each other and sharing the burden back and forth. We're incredible. Hats off to us. 10/10, no notes. (Actually, we have some notes....)

Finally, thank you to every queer athlete out there, whether you're out or still in the closet. You are incredible. You are brave. You are strong. You are not alone. We'll always be your cheerleaders, your coaches, your teammates, and your friends. We're there on the sidelines, in the bleachers, on the shore, at the boards, and at the finish line. Right down to the very last buzzer. We're rooting for you.